▶ Understanding and Managing IT Outsourcing

DOI: 10.1057/9781137497321.0001

Other Palgrave Pivot titles

Keiichi Kubota and Hitoshi Takehara: Reform and Price Discovery at the Tokyo Stock Exchange: From 1990 to 2012

Emanuele Rossi and Rok Stepic: Infrastructure Project Finance and Project Bonds in Europe: Infrastructure Project Finance and Project Bonds in Europe

Annalisa Furia: The Foreign Aid Regime: Gift-Giving, States and Global Dis/Order

C. J. T. Talar and Lawrence F. Barmann (editors): Roman Catholic Modernists Confront the Great War

Bernard Kelly: Military Internees, Prisoners of War and the Irish State during the Second World War

James Raven: Lost Mansions: Essays on the Destruction of the Country House

Luigino Bruni: A Lexicon of Social Well-Being

Michael Byron: Submission and Subjection in Leviathan: Good Subjects in the Hobbesian Commonwealth

Andrew Szanajda: The Allies and the German Problem, 1941–1949: From Cooperation to Alternative Settlement

Joseph E. Stiglitz and Refet S. Gürkaynak: Taming Capital Flows: Capital Account Management in an Era of Globalization

Steffen Mau: Inequality, Marketization and the Majority Class: Why Did the European Middle Classes Accept Neo-Liberalism?

Amelia Lambelet and Raphael Berthele: Age and Foreign Language Learning in School

Justin Robertson: Localizing Global Finance: The Rise of Western-Style Private Equity in China

Isabel Dulfano: Indigenous Feminist Narratives: I/We: Wo(men) of An(Other) Way

Stefan Lund: School Choice, Ethnic Divisions, and Symbolic Boundaries

Daniel Wirls: The Federalist Papers and Institutional Power: In American Political Development

Marcus Morgan and Patrick Baert: Conflict in the Academy: A Study in the Sociology of Intellectuals

Robyn Henderson and Karen Noble: Professional Learning, Induction and Critical Reflection: Building Workforce Capacity in Education

Graeme Kirkpatrick : The Formation of Gaming Culture: UK Gaming Magazines, 1981–1995

Candice C. Carter: Social Education for Peace: Foundations, Teaching, and Curriculum for Visionary Learning

DOI: 10.1057/9781137497321.0001

palgrave▶**pivot**

Understanding and Managing IT Outsourcing: A Partnership Approach

Surja Datta
Oxford Brookes University, UK

and

Neil Oschlag-Michael
Ase, Denmark

DOI: 10.1057/9781137497321.0001

First published 2015 by
PALGRAVE MACMILLAN

Palgrave Macmillan in the UK is an imprint of Macmillan Publishers Limited, registered in England, company number 785998, of Houndmills, Basingstoke, Hampshire RG21 6XS.

Palgrave Macmillan in the US is a division of St Martin's Press LLC, 175 Fifth Avenue, New York, NY 10010.

Palgrave Macmillan is the global academic imprint of the above companies and has companies and representatives throughout the world.

Palgrave® and Macmillan® are registered trademarks in the United States, the United Kingdom, Europe and other countries.

ISBN: 978–1–137–49731–4 EPUB
ISBN: 978–1–137–49732–1 PDF
ISBN: 978–1–137–49730–7 Hardback

A catalogue record for this book is available from the British Library.

A catalog record for this book is available from the Library of Congress.

www.palgrave.com/pivot

DOI: 10.1057/9781137497321

Surja would like to dedicate this book to his parents. Neil would like to dedicate this book to his son, Uriah, his nephew, Ian, and his nieces, Ria and Isobel.

DOI: 10.1057/9781137497321.0001

Contents

DOI: 10.1057/9781137497321.0001

DOI: 10.1057/9781137497321.0001

List of Figures

DOI: 10.1057/9781137497321.0002

List of Tables

About the Authors

Surja Datta received his doctorate from Bristol Business School, University of the West of England. Surja also holds an MBA from Strathclyde University and an MA in Applied Social Research from the University of the West of England. Surja's research interests include innovation and outsourcing. He was earlier involved in a European Commission project that developed business and innovation models for environment monitoring services in Europe.

▶ **Neil Oschlag-Michael** is a strategy, management and technology consultant. He has extensive global experience in a range of strategy, business transformation, outsourcing and development roles, working at businesses, consultancies and vendors. He holds an MBA from Oxford Brookes University and his research interests include innovation, transformation and outsourcing.

DOI: 10.1057/9781137497321.0004

Introduction

Datta, Surja and Neil Oschlag-Michael. *Understanding and Managing IT Outsourcing: A Partnership Approach.* Basingstoke: Palgrave Macmillan, 2015. DOI: 10.1057/9781137497321.0005.

▶

Outsourcing in general and IT outsourcing in particular have grown exponentially over the recent years. The academic literature on the topic has also burgeoned, exploring and investigating the phenomenon from different theoretical perspectives such as transaction cost economics, organizational knowledge, competitive business strategies, and value chain and so on. In conjunction with the academic literature, there has also been growth in the practitioner literature around outsourcing. But there is an absence of overlap between the two streams of literature. The practitioner-oriented literature by and large ignores academic theories while its scholarly counterpart focuses mainly on theoretical constructs that explains the 'make or buy' decision but provides little in terms of heuristics that practitioners can use in real business situations.

The main objective of this book is to meet this gap between theory and practice. Two central themes run through this research and they relate to uncertainty and partnership in outsourcing relationships. It is argued in this research that to understand the complexities of outsourcing and to manage the process effectively, it is essential to understand the multi-dimensional nature of uncertainties associated with it. The argument is put forward that a partnership approach is desirable in outsourcing relationships that are characterized with high uncertainty.

The book is structured in the following way. Chapter 1 introduces the topic of IT outsourcing, its evolution over time and the key theoretical lens through which the phenomenon has been explored and investigated up till now. In Chapter 2, the multidimensional nature of uncertainty is unpacked and its relation with outsourcing is established. Chapter 3 focuses on trust and partnerships and their nature and role in outsourcing relationships. In Chapter 4, a conceptual framework is developed which brings together the themes of uncertainty and trust and elucidates the interrelationships between them. This chapter also identifies the two generic approaches to outsourcing. Chapter 5 contains paradigmatic case studies which illustrate the presence and absence of uncertainty and trust in outsourcing relationships. In Conclusions, the main conceptual and empirical findings of the study are highlighted.

1
IT Outsourcing

Datta, Surja and Neil Oschlag-Michael. *Understanding and Managing IT Outsourcing: A Partnership Approach.* Basingstoke: Palgrave Macmillan, 2015. DOI: 10.1057/9781137497321.0006.

▶

The aim in this section is to provide an introduction to IT outsourcing and set the context for the issues of uncertainties, trust and partnerships, all of which are examined in detail in the subsequent chapters.

1.1   Introduction

Grover et al. (1996) provide a simple definition of IT outsourcing, namely *the practice of turning over part or all of an organization's information system functions to an external service provider.* This definition addresses the issue of the terms IT outsourcing and information system outsourcing (ISO), being used interchangeably.

Given that outsourcing is often mistaken for offshoring, it is worth noting that offshoring, within the context of outsourcing, is when some or all of the service provided is delivered from a foreign location. In offshored outsourcing complexity of services increases, as does uncertainty and the need for management control and trust in the outsourcing relationship (Gottschalk and Solli-Saether, 2005).

IT outsourcing roots can be traced to the traditional time sharing and professional services of the 1960s and 1970s (Grover et al., 1996). *The 1970s marked the beginning of the application package concept and the decline of processing services and the 1980s marked the arrival of low-cost minicomputers and PCs* and *focus shifted to IT-supported vertical integration during this decade* (Kim et al., 2003). IT outsourcing *has been widely publicized ever since Kodak's landmark decision to outsource the bulk of their IT functions in the late 1980s* (Willcocks and Lacity, 2009). In the early 1990s *interest in outsourcing resurfaced with network and telecommunication management, distributed systems integration, application development and systems operations* (Kim et al., 2003). At that stage the importance, nature and diversity of IT outsourcing was changing and companies begin to take a more strategic and proactive approach to it (Grover et al., 1996). IT outsourcing has grown rapidly since then and with the recent advent of the cloud, which refers to both the applications delivered as services over the Internet and the hardware and systems software in the data centres that provide those services (Armbrust et al., 2009) and Armbrust et al. (2009) are supported widely in their suggestion that the long-held dream of computing as a utility has the potential to transform IT outsourcing.

While business process outsourcing (BPO) is recognized as a separate domain, boundaries between BPO and IT outsourcing are difficult to define, especially when the underlying IT services are also outsourced to the same service provider. This issue is also complicated by the fact that

DOI: 10.1057/9781137497321.0006

some business processes have become IT services and certain definitions of IT outsourcing include 'IT-enabled business processes' (Gartner, 2013). BPO is also growing rapidly and some forecasts expect it to overshadow IT outsourcing (Oshri et al., 2009).

While Gartner (2013), an IT research and advisory consultancy, provides a simple classification of IT outsourcing functions, IT-enabled business processes, application services and infrastructure services, there are several views of what IT services and IT outsourcing functions comprise. Some suggestions for classification of IT outsourcing functional areas are simple and include project management, applications development, applications management, data centre operations, infrastructure acquisition, infrastructure maintenance, systems development and systems maintenance (Fish and Seydel, 2006). Classification is not made easier by the variance in service offerings between service providers. TCS, a large global service provider, for instance, lists over a dozen service offerings on its website (tcs.com, 2014) whereas IBM, another large global service provider, lists over two dozen service offerings on its website (ibm.com, 2014).

The same issue applies to IT outsourcing engagement options, some of which can be reconciled into two main types: total outsourcing and selective outsourcing (Willcocks and Lacity, 2009). In total outsourcing all or most (usually more than 80 per cent) of the IT budget for IT assets, leases, staff and management responsibility is transferred to an external IT provider (Dibbern et al., 2004; Willcocks and Lacity, 2009). A variation of this option is when a firm becomes more business oriented and outsources the entire business outcome, instead of focusing on the service process (Patel and Aran, 2005). In this scenario, partnerships become more relevant as sourcing options can include partnering, mergers and acquisitions (Patel and Aran, 2005). In selective outsourcing only selected IT functions are outsourced to single or multiple vendors and most IT functions are provided internally (Willcocks and Lacity, 2009).

Partnerships and collaborations are also relevant for selective outsourcing and certain models; for instance the Arana 'Matrix of outsourcing models under different scenarios' (cited in Patel and Aran, 2005) calls for it explicitly when there is reasonable probability of an activity becoming a competitive advantage and when a company's internal capabilities are weaker or similar to those of its competitors (Patel and Aran, 2005). Interestingly, Patel and Aran (2005) argue that the degree of competitive advantage from the outsourcing initiative should determine the strength of the relationship needed.

DOI: 10.1057/9781137497321.0006

Grover et al. (1996) are not alone in suggesting that the underlying motivation for IT outsourcing can be explained with two models: the resource-based view (RBV) and transaction cost economics (TCE). The RBV theory posits that a firm's capabilities are critical for its achieving competitive advantage and that firms can fill gaps in their existing capabilities or develop them further by acquiring resources and capabilities from the market. TCE posits that firms can reduce costs by outsourcing activities to exploit market economies of scale and specialization. Research suggests that TCE is the most important motivator for IT outsourcing (Lacity et al., 2009).

TCE and RBV can be used to identify resources or services which are best suited for outsourcing due to the nature of their attributes. TCE advocates outsourcing when services are associated with low asset specificity, low uncertainty, high substitutability or low frequency of use. RBV advocates outsourcing when in-house services are not valuable, common, imitable or substitutable or when the market provides services which are valuable, rare, non-imitable or non-substitutable.

While outsourcing is well aligned with TCE, it does not necessarily help a firm achieve competitive advantage. The underlying strategic motivation for IT outsourcing can also be explained by RBV and dynamic capabilities, which are 'the firm's ability to integrate, build, and reconfigure internal and external competences to address rapidly changing environments' (Teece et al., 1997) in order to achieve new forms of competitive advantage. 'Instead of capabilities, the organization has the alternative to go for the outsourcing of services or solutions' (Patel and Aran, 2005), which ironically is the rationale for acquiring dynamic capabilities in the first place, demonstrating how well aligned RBV is with outsourcing to achieve competitive advantage.

There are also other strategic reasons in strategic partnerships, like those suggested by Ansoff (1987), and IT outsourcing can be a means to gain access to new markets and segments or to produce new or innovative products or services faster than its competitors, thereby providing a means of competitive advantage. Achieving cost leadership, a generic strategy suggested by Porter (1980), due to IT outsourcing is unlikely, given that IT outsourcing services are plentiful and easily available. Increasing IT system commoditization (Willcocks and Lacity, 2009) makes differentiation increasingly difficult; a better explanation from this school is that IT outsourcing enables a company to 'focus on core' competencies and that IT outsourcing's only contribution is improving

DOI: 10.1057/9781137497321.0006

operational efficiency. Nevertheless, when TCE-based outsourcing contributes to an underlying cost-leadership business strategy, outsourcing relationships can be a means of achieving competitive advantage.

Despite its ubiquitous use in IT outsourcing 'sourcing strategy' rarely has anything in common with business strategy. Once a business strategy or initiative has been defined, i.e. 'what is to be done', sourcing strategy is the next step, i.e., 'who will do it' (Patel and Aran, 2005).

Willcocks and Lacity (2009) argue that IT outsourcing success should be assessed based on the extent to which organizations achieving their desired nominated outcomes during the period when those outcomes were being pursued. There are several studies on IT outsourcing outcomes and Willcocks and Lacity (2009) provide a detailed, compiled list of categorized IT outsourcing expectations. These include financial expectations (reduce costs, improve cost control and restructure IT budgets), business expectations (return to core, facilitate mergers and acquisitions and enable start-ups), technical expectations (improve technical service, access technical talent, and access to new technologies) and political expectations (prove efficiency, justify new resources, duplicate success, expose exaggerated claims and eliminate troublesome function).

Despite this framework, issues remain with assessing IT outsourcing outcomes and success: there is a lack of an accepted success construct, the definition and meaning of success differs and desired outcomes can change over time (Willcocks and Lacity, 2009). Grover et al. (1996) also provide a framework to evaluate success and introduce the notion that partnership elements are important variables for outsourcing. Their research shows that service quality and partnership elements such as trust, cooperation, and communication are important for outsourcing success.

Given the alignment of RBV with outsourcing it is not surprising that some scholars, Feeny et al. (2005), Oshri et al. (2009) and Willcocks and Lacity (2006) for instance, stress the importance of vendor capabilities. Feeny et al. (2005) identify 12 vendor capabilities (Planning & Contracting, Organisational Design, Governance, Customer Development, Leadership, Business Management, Programme Management, Process Re-engineering, Sourcing, Domain Expertise, Behaviour Management and Technology Exploitation), which they advise companies to assess. Willcocks and Lacity (2006) group these together in three key vendor competences. Interestingly, one of these is the 'relationship competency',

DOI: 10.1057/9781137497321.0006

which is based on a vendor's willingness to consider a client's values and goals while implementing their delivery model, confirming the importance and desirability of what appears to be a type of 'partnership' competency.

The cloud is transforming the IT sector and IT outsourcing may only become far more pervasive and extensive. By lowering transaction costs, IT allows big chunks of the economy to reshape and the IT sector looks like a pyramid where economies of scale rule the bottom and creativity and agility are desired at the top (Economist, 2014). Progress is rapid and some services that it took a company six months to get up and running in the 1990s take a few weeks today via the internet and command a lower fee (Economist, 2014).

Deloitte, a consultancy, is not alone in discussing the notion of a 'virtual vendor' and suggesting that the cloud may make business models such as 'vendor as broker' and 'vendor as retailer' economically feasible (Deloitte, 2013). This is very interesting from a partnership perspective as it suggests longer supplier chains and end-service providers with whom relationships may only weaken. However, nothing is certain and market dynamics will determine whether cloud sourcing will be the demise of traditional outsourcing or will result in next-generation outsourcing (Gartner, 2014).

1.2   Risks and uncertainties

There are several studies on IT outsourcing risks; Oshri et al. (2009) and Civilis (2013) provide compiled categorized lists of them. Oshri et al.'s (2009) risk list includes business risks (no overall cost savings, poor quality and late deliverables), social risks (cultural differences, holiday and religious calendar differences), logistical risks (time-zone challenges, managing remote teams and coordinating travel), workforce risks (supplier-employee turnover, supplier-employee burnout, inexperienced supplier employees, poor communication and skills of supplier employees), legal risks (inefficient or ineffective judicial system at offshore location, intellectual property rights infringement, export restrictions, inflexible labour laws, difficulty obtaining visas and changes in tax laws, inflexible contracts and breaches in security or privacy) and political risks (backlash from internal staff, perceived as unpatriotic, political instability with or within the offshore country).

DOI: 10.1057/9781137497321.0006

Suggestions for risk lists can overlap and Civilis's (2013) compilation of risks from outsourcing studies includes organizational risks (poor service quality, loss of knowledge, rigid collaboration, poor employee morale and loss of innovation), financial risks (hidden cost, overstated benefits, loss of revenue), contractual risks (poor contract management, wrong partner selection, power shift to supplier, lock-in with supplier) and environmental risks (legal obstacles, distance, negative press and creating a competitor).

Risks can also be classified into structural and operational risks (Oshri et al., 2009). Operational risk is high when processes are opaque or when they cannot be codified and measured. Structural risk arises when the relationship between clients and suppliers may not work as expected (Oshri et al., 2009). Aron and Singh (2005, cited in Oshri et al., 2009) suggest that captive and internal functions are better suited than outsourcing when there is a high structural or operational risk. This is a common approach and explains why basic infrastructure services are so widespread in outsourcing. Refer to Figure 1.1 for examples of IT services associated with increasing levels of codifiability.

While this suggestion does mitigate risk, it has the downside that it may end up excluding outsourcing in areas which may provide the greatest benefits: innovation and competitive advantage, perhaps even at a lower cost and higher service level than being able to deliver these functions internally.

The ability for outsourcing to spur innovation is documented. Lacity and Willcocks (2014) argue that most successful companies concentrate

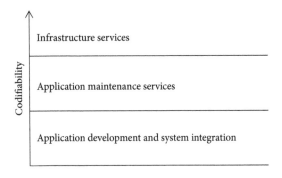

FIGURE 1.1 *Examples of common IT services with increasing levels of codifiability*
Source: Authors' own.

DOI: 10.1057/9781137497321.0006

less on cost savings and more on innovation. In a study they conducted on a successful and innovative BPO relationship, they identified gain sharing as an important element and the service provider partner is cited as saying that 'the key message is a spirit of partnership that I don't think exists in the other engagements that I've come across' (Lacity and Willcocks, 2014).

It is often assumed that risks and uncertainties refer to the same issue and it is necessary to make the distinction between these terms. Knight (1921) suggested that risks are situations where a particular outcome can be assigned probabilities. In other words, risk is uncertainty that can be insured against, as the quantification of risk through the assignment of probabilities to different possible outcomes lies at the heart of insurance. Uncertainty on the other hand refers to situations where it is impossible to assign any probabilities to possible outcomes: uncertainties are uninsurable and not quantifiable. There is little research on uncertainties through an IT-outsourcing lens. However, uncertainties are an important theme in this study and are examined in more detail in Chapter 2.

DOI: 10.1057/9781137497321.0006

2

Uncertainties in Outsourcing

Datta, Surja and Neil Oschlag-Michael. *Understanding and Managing IT Outsourcing: A Partnership Approach.* Basingstoke: Palgrave Macmillan, 2015. DOI: 10.1057/9781137497321.0007.

▶

The aim of this chapter is to identify and understand the various forms of uncertainties that surround the outsourcing decision and the outsourcing process.

2.1   Introduction

Uncertainty can be generally thought of as the difficulty firms face when predicting the future. In the outsourcing context, this can thought of as the uncertainty about the outcome of the decision to outsource. Transaction cost economics (TCE) holds that uncertainty of transaction costs is central to the decision to 'make or buy' (Williamson, 1985). Transaction costs are the costs of accessing the market mechanism (Coase, 1937) which includes costs such as costs of a search for a suitable supplier, costs of monitoring the relationship and costs of enforcement of contracts. High uncertainty of such transaction costs leads to market failure and results in hierarchy (Williamson, 1979). It is argued in TCE that the majority of the activities that a firm performs concern technologically separable interfaces and thus can be organized through alternate governance structures, market or hierarchy. It is the relative efficiency of the governance structures that decide whether a transaction is produced internally or is procured from the market.

Granovetter (1985) points out that human action has been traditionally explained in two very different ways which he describes as undersocialized and oversocialized concepts of human action. The under-socialized view of human action sees it as taken by rational atomistic actors, albeit the rationality is accepted as 'bounded'. Social ties here do not, in general, affect the economic decision making and if any anything are seen as causing frictional drag that distorts competitive markets. Oversocialized concept on the other hand, sees such action governed by social norms and practices and thus scope for choice by human agents is severely limited. Trying to understand uncertainty through these two concepts would lead to very different interpretations. With assumption of *homo economicus* (rational economic man), uncertainty is about lack of complete information, while in *homo socius* (social man), uncertainty is about deviation from social norms and practices. However, there have also been attempts to integrate social ties in explanation of economic action.

Rather than seeing social ties as an unnecessary drag on competitive markets, these are seen as resources for purposive action (Coleman, 1986). In this paradigm, choices are real and these are about choices in social relations (Lin, 2001). Here, both action and structure are important and they influence each other. Structure shapes both opportunities and constraints, but choices made within these opportunities and constraints also affect the structure.

If we acknowledge that social capital has economic value, just as in the case of physical and financial capital, the question it begets is how such capital contributes to economic action. Interorganizational trust has been directly linked with social capital. Social ties engender trust, which in turn helps in avoidance of opportunistic behaviour. Network governance, which has been seen as a particular governance mechanism where vertical de-aggregation is achieved through interdependency amongst organizations, is said to be characterized by high level of trust (Jones et al., 1997). Besides engendering trust, social networks have been found to facilitate search for new information. Granovetter (1973) points out that weak ties are better for accessing new information, as the information which circulates within strong ties are often redundant. The issues of trust and search are dealt with in more detail later in the chapter; suffice to say here that social networks and social capital it represents are important in explanation of economic action and in the context of this research needs to be included in understanding uncertainties related to outsourcing. This is in accordance with the view put forward by Jones et al. (1997), that integrating transaction cost theory with social network theory provides a useful way to understand economic action.

Further, as Rangan (2000) argues, social networks are particularly useful in explanation of economic action that includes search and deliberation. Search is seen as the exploration for potential exchange partners while deliberation involves uncertainty related to the behaviour of the potential partners. Both these issues are central to outsourcing. Yet another strand of literature on social capital emphasizes the role it has in organizational knowledge production. Nahapiet and Ghoshal (1998) argue that social capital leads to production of intellectual capital in organizations and this follows similar suggestions made earlier by Kogut and Zander (1992) and Spender (1996). These authors make the common point that organizations are particularly well suited to create collective knowledge collaboration and exchange.

To conclude this part of the discussion on the role of social capital in organizational context, the literature suggests that social capital broadly influences the following: a) Interorganizational trust, b) Search for network partners and c) Organizational knowledge production. Further,

DOI: 10.1057/9781137497321.0007

it seems that different kinds of networks have different comparative advantages; while strong network ties facilitate trust, weak ties help to bring in fresh information and organizational ties help in collective collaboration that leads to organizational knowledge.

Before trying to specify the various kinds of uncertainties relating to outsourcing, it is perhaps useful to specify what is meant by uncertainty in the context of this research. Neo-classical economics looks at uncertainty as a situation where it is difficult to make probabilistic assumptions about the future. It is Knight (1921) who made the distinction between uncertainty and risk by stating that uncertainty becomes risk when it is becomes insurable, which in turn is possible when one can assign probabilities to possible future outcomes. The idea behind this is that *homo economicus* is a utility maximizing entity. Some of the problems with this approach have been pointed out by other economists, notably Simon (1955) who argues that boundedness of human cognition is the main constraint of humans being aware of all possible preference rankings and hence the problem of optimizing. Instead of optimizing, uncertainty is reduced by carrying out a local search instead of a global search, the outcome of which can be sub-optimal. Cognitive psychologists have suggested that we tend to use heuristics to express our belief about an uncertain outcome (Tversky and Kahneman, 1974). These heuristics, often useful, can also lead to systematic errors. Consider the following example, how heuristics can lead to over- and underestimation of an uncertain event (reproduced from Tversky and Kahneman, 1974)

> The subjective assessment of probability resembles the subjective assessment of physical quantities such as distance or size. These judgements are all based on data of limited validity, which are processed according to heuristic rules. For example, the apparent distance of an object is determined in part by its clarity. The more sharply the object is seen, the closer it appears to be. This rule has some validity, because in any given scene the more distant objects are seen less sharply than nearer objects. However, the reliance on this rule leads to systematic errors in the estimation of distance. Specifically, distances are often overestimated when visibility is poor because the contours of objects are blurred. On the other hand, distances are often underestimated when visibility is good because the objects are seen sharply. Thus, the reliance on clarity as an indication of distance leads to common biases.

TCE continues in this vein to propose that institutions like firms are governance mechanisms for reducing market uncertainty. The role of hierarchy in reducing market uncertainty has also been emphasized by

DOI: 10.1057/9781137497321.0007

Chandler (1977) in his largely historical perspective of the rise in visible hand (in contradistinction from invisible hand of markets as thought by Adam Smith) of managerial hierarchy in the late nineteenth century which continued till mid-twentieth century. The concept of bounded rationality suggests that the governance choice by firms may not be optimal as the decision is based on certain heuristic principles which are prone to biases.

Although, theoretical lenses like TCE and the concept of bounded rationality help in explaining existence of social institutions like firms, it does not fully recognize the role of social networks and ties in human actions. Uncertainties, constraints and opportunities that arise from economic action being embedded in social relations are therefore missed from both the neo-classical and new institutional economic analysis. From sociological viewpoint, uncertainty has been re-conceptualized as double contingency (Beckert, 1996). Ego is uncertain about his alter ego's action while alter ego is uncertain about ego's action. It is important to note that the main difference between new institutional economics and management literature that emphasizes the importance the role of social relations is not on the nature of market uncertainty itself but on how normatively firms manage this uncertainty. While the former empha-sizes the role of formal sanctions and hierarchy in reducing uncertainty, the latter highlights the role of informal sanctions, social networks and reciprocity.

Trying to integrate the concept of bounded rationality and social capi-tal in explaining governance choice by firms, Uzzi (1997) has suggested that firms do a limited search for network partners that is constrained by the social ties in which the firm is embedded. The point here is that rationality is bounded both by cognitive and social constraints. The outsourcing process thus can be seen to be affected by changing patterns of cognitive as well as social capital of the firm.

One way to look at outsourcing is to see it as a 'make' and then 'buy' decision rather than a 'make or buy' decision. The benefit of looking at outsourcing in such a fashion is to recognize the organizational history of 'making' an activity. While it may be conceptually correct to assume that transactions performed over technologically separable interfaces are candidates for the 'make or buy' decision, it is important to note that the organizational history of an activity brings its own set of dynamics and uncertainties. Producing an activity internally for a period of time leads to building up organizational capabilities required to perform the activity. These capabilities would include both intangibles such as

DOI: 10.1057/9781137497321.0007

organizational knowledge and tangible resources like physical infrastructure and human resources.

The decision to outsource also leads to uncertainty about how to manage such resources. One way to deal with the issue, and this is often adopted by organizations, is not to assign any economic value to such capabilities and think of it as redundant in wake of procuring the activity from the market. But another way of thinking is that any set of organizational capabilities provides strategic options for organizations (Bowman and Hurry, 1993). Real options such as organizational capabilities have real economic value that can be of strategic use for firms. Thus, an outsourcing decision has the added uncertainty of dealing with existing organizational capabilities.

As mentioned earlier, uncertainty as conceptualized under TCE relates to uncertainty of transaction costs (Williamson, 1975). Higher the uncertainty, higher is the possibility that a firm would opt to produce an activity internally. The argument is that high uncertainty causes market failure and forces firms to choose hierarchy. But high uncertainty should not automatically lead to hierarchy; after all, high uncertainty can potentially lead to rich pickings as it can eventually turn out that actual transaction costs incurred turn out to be very low. High uncertainty can lead a firm to organize an activity within hierarchy only when it is accompanied by certain behavioural assumptions. In TCE, there is an automatic assumption of opportunistic behaviour, which means that parties involved will behave opportunistically if it is possible for them to get away with it. This also signifies a lack of trust, as trust is normally seen as a resource that impedes opportunistic behaviour in situations where such behaviour is possible (Lewicki and Bunker, 1996). Some have, however, conceptualized the behaviour under TCE as a different kind of trust: Calculus-based trust (Maguire et al., 2001) which is based on the calculation of other party's behaviour.

In this study, trust is seen as an uncertainty-reducing mechanism (Lane and Bachmann, 1996). Firms often interact with suppliers with whom they trust. Newness of suppliers can be a source of uncertainty as without a history of past interactions, firms may find it hard to predict supplier behaviour. However, somewhat paradoxically, new suppliers are also sought to reduce uncertainties. This is done mainly to diversify supply sources and also perhaps for legitimacy concerns (Beckman et al., 2004). Notwithstanding the need for certain newness amongst supplier base, trust as a mechanism for reducing uncertainty of opportunistic

DOI: 10.1057/9781137497321.0007

behaviour and lubricating the relationship between buyer and supplier features strongly in interorganizational literature. Trust, it has been argued, occurs primarily at inter-personal level rather than at interorganizational level (Bachman, 2001). The incremental nature of trust has also been emphasized by several academic observers (Lewicki and Bunker, 1996; Huxham and Vangen, 2003).

One issue that is often left at an implicit level in the analysis of trust is the role of geographical proximity in the generation of interorganizational trust. Most of the empirical work on trust is carried out in a context where the organizations and organizational actors are in geographical proximity. Is geographical proximity a necessary condition for emergence of network governance or is it something that has happened due to other factors, proximity amongst actors being not critical for the process? Recent years have seen phenomenal growth in procurement of services from geographical dispersed regions. This provides a context to explore how interorganizational trust emerges in absence of geographical proximity.

As seen from the earlier discussion, outsourcing is more of a 'make' and then 'buy' decision rather than just a 'make or buy'. The history of making an activity internally also makes the context important in the outsourcing decision. Organizations are networks of activity that are intricately linked often in a manner that is unconscious to individual agents (Krackhardt, 1990). Decoupling an activity within these networks of activity is an exercise that has implications beyond the relative efficiency of making the activity internally vis-à-vis procuring the same from the market. An activity can be thought of as a pattern of behaviour between organizational actors to perform tasks. These patterns of behaviour are often unconscious even to agents who are performing them (Nelson and Winter, 1982). But organization routines, as these patterns of behaviours are sometimes referred to in the literature, have great organizational value in terms of stability, speed and reliability of task outcome (Cohen and Bacdayan, 1996). The organizational routines constitute organizational knowledge and as Spender (1996) suggests it is the collective knowledge, which is social and implicit, that is often the source of the competitive advantage of firms. This is similar to the view expressed by Kogut and Zander (1992) that the source of competitive advantage is embedded in informal networks within the organization in a tacit fashion. Loss of competitive advantage has been cited as one of the main risks of outsourcing (Quinn and Hilmer, 1994), which would suggest that there is a possibility of loss of social, implicit knowledge through the outsourcing process.

The context specificity of organizational routines has been well documented (for a review of literature on organizational routines, see Becker, 2004) which points out the difficulty of replicating existing organizational routines in a new context. Outsourcing is a conscious decision, taken by an agent or a group of agents, which affects a largely unconscious network of activity.

The unconscious network or informal network as it is sometimes called (Krackhardt and Hanson, 1993) is often different from the formal organizational structure, yet it is the formal structure that is codified or readily available to the agent(s) responsible for the outsourcing decision. As Quinn (1999) points out, the outsourcing decision is increasingly taken at a senior-management level (Chief Executive Officer, Chief Finance Officer, Chief Operational Officer) as it is this section of the managerial hierarchy that is seen as being responsible for maximizing shareholder value and outsourcing is increasingly seen as a tool for such an effort.

However, as Spender (1996) suggests, ex ante it is not clear why the senior management should automatically be more cognizant of the dynamics of organizational knowledge than the rest of the firm. Many academic observers in fact point to the other direction, that is, senior management is often unaware of the informal networks that operate within organizations they manage (Krackhardt and Hanson, 1993).

It is evident from this discussion that a decision taken solely on the basis of relative efficiency of producing an activity within hierarchy or procuring the same through the market will miss out on important issues that have a bearing on the decision. An activity within a network activity is not performed in isolation nor are the organizational actors involved in performing the activity involved solely in the production of the activity. Thus, uncertainty about which activities to outsource goes beyond market uncertainty of transaction costs associated with such activities.

Recent years have seen tremendous growth in outsourcing from geographically dispersed regions. This growth has been typically explained in terms of low labour cost in the countries from which the services are being procured. This explanation does not explain much. For example, it is not clear why there is huge concentration of locations from where services are being procured (a lot of the services are procured from a single country, India) and not from other locations where labour costs

DOI: 10.1057/9781137497321.0007

are equally low or sometimes even lower. A rather less obvious question would be why the growth in offshore outsourcing, though exponential, is not even higher? Advances in telecommunication technologies have ensured that there are few technological barriers to firms sourcing services globally. As individuals we procure goods and services all over the world or communicate with our near and dear ones who are based on other side of the world with low-cost technologies like Skype. Yet firms show remarkable reluctance to procure services from geographically dispersed regions, even when few technological barriers remain and there is a clear labour cost arbitrage. Thus, offshore outsourcing provides an ideal setting to explore in depth some of the concepts touched upon earlier.

Intuitively, one senses that uncertainty is greater when services are procured offshore. But what leads to this heightened sense of uncertainty? From the new institutional economic perspective, one can say that the basis of the heightened sense of uncertainty lies in the different institutional norms that the buyer and seller face in the case of offshore outsourcing. Institutions, following North's (1990) argument, are the rules of the game, both formal and informal. In the case of domestic outsourcing, the institutional setting in which the buyer and seller operate is the same, while in offshore outsourcing it is different. As pointed out by North, the primary purpose of institutions is to reduce uncertainty in transactions, but this of course implies a familiarity with the institutions of both the formal and informal types. Firms that are spatially located in geographical locations that are separated by large distances would have familiarity with local institutions but would have relatively less knowledge about institutions that its partner firm is embedded in. One can see how such information asymmetry about institutions leads to a heightened sense of uncertainty in offshore transactions. But the uncertainty in offshore outsourcing of services goes beyond the issue of unfamiliarity with distant institutions. The level of uncertainty also has something to do with the nature of the transactions involved. To explain this point more precisely, one needs to borrow heavily on North's (1990) explanation of transaction cost theory of exchange. That transaction costs play an important role in the 'make or buy' decision was pointed out a long time ago by Coase (1937), but what has been less clear is what exactly makes transactions costs 'costly'. Coase gave a general description of transaction cost by stating that it is the cost of accessing the market mechanism. North (1990) further unpacks this concept of transaction cost by pointing out that there are two main components of such costs,

DOI: 10.1057/9781137497321.0007

namely the cost of measurement of the attributes of the goods and services to be procured and the cost of monitoring the relationship. When we buy goods and services, we do so because we derive certain utility out of the attributes of the goods and services purchased. For example, a car has certain attributes like colour, speed, interior design and so on that are valued by us when we buy the car. Any service will also have similar attributes attached to it. When we go to a restaurant, we not only value the food but also the décor, the attentiveness of the service, the level of hygiene maintained and so on. As North (1990) explains, the value of the exchange is then the value of different attributes lumped together into discrete goods and services. The problem in exchange is, however, the presence of information asymmetry between the buyer and seller, which results in one party being more aware of the real value of these attributes than the other. The seller of the goods and services is typically more aware of the value of the attributes than the buyer, and the buyer needs to measure the value of attributes and thus has to incur costs to do this. North does not distinguish between goods and services in terms of ease of measuring the value of different attributes. The distinction between goods and service measurement is well documented in other unrelated literature especially in the area of service management. The distinction between goods and services in terms of measurement of the attributes can be made in terms of visibility of the attributes, tangibility, temporal lag between production and consumption, all of which contribute to the problem of measurement of service quality. So we can say here that uncertainty related to measurement of service attributes would in general be more than that in the case of tangible goods.

The other dimension of transaction costs, namely the cost of monitoring a transactional relationship, on the other hand depends primarily on the behaviour of the agents that are involved in the transaction. If the agents display untrustworthy behaviour, the costs of monitoring would be high whereas if they are trustworthy this cost will be relatively lesser.

The uncertainty of trustworthiness of the transactional partners has been an issue since trade expanded beyond closely knit primitive society (North, 1991). The issue was brought into even more prominence once long distance trade was established. As North points out, early traders usually sent a close relative with merchandise to reduce the risk of defection, but as such trade expanded, this method of risk mitigation suffered from its obvious limitations. This, in turn, helped in building institutions that facilitated impersonal third party enforcement of contractual

DOI: 10.1057/9781137497321.0007

agreements to cater for loss on strong interpersonal ties. How does the modern world of long-distance service trading differ from the old world of long-distance goods trading?

At one level, one can safely say that the opportunity for building interpersonal ties across large geographical distances is much higher in modern times than that which existed in the early days of long-distance trade. Innovation in transport and communication technologies has led to greater physical and social interaction between people located in different parts of the world. Of course, this does not imply that the world now has turned into one big, close-knit society that lessens the need for formal institutions to enforce contracts. The complexity of the environment entails that such institutions are a necessary pre-condition for cooperative activity between partners that are both spatially and temporally separated. However, it is also important to note that modern trade in services takes place in a context where it is entirely possible that the partners involved have prior social ties. Such social ties can encourage cooperative behaviour much more than the mere presence of formal institutions to deter defection. It is tentatively suggested here that the presence of prior social ties will encourage cooperative behaviour between partners that are spatially and temporally separated as this reduces the risk for' opportunistic behaviour by one of the partners.

To summarize this part of the discussion, we can say that uncertainty in offshore outsourcing of services arises out of three distinct issues. First, it arises out of unfamiliarity with distant institutions. Second, the difficulty in assessing the trustworthiness of partners located in distant locales contributes to the uncertainty; and third, difficulties in measurement of service attributes add to the uncertainty.

Organizational trust has been generally explored in a context where organizations and interorganizational actors are in geographical proximity to each other. If geographical proximity is critical in engendering trust, what can explain the geographical dispersion of service procurement that we are witnessing now? What leads to the emergence of trust between organizations that are both spatially and temporally separated?

'Network' is seen as a governance mechanism that is distinct from both market and hierarchy (Piore, 1992). Network governance is characterized by high level of trust and interdependence between firms which allows for vertical de-aggregation (Jones et al., 1997). But network governance, that is, small and medium-sized firms having a high degree of interdependency has been typically observed when firms are in close geographical proximity. Regional clusters, as observed in the Silicon Valley and Keiretsu ties in Japan, are examples of network governance. However, in the case of offshore outsourcing, we have seen the emergence of network governance across national boundaries and huge geographical distances. Big firms have of course taken advantage of low labour cost and have either set up their own shop or set up relations with third party service providers, but along with multinational firms, small and medium-sized firms across nations are interacting in a way that can be characterized as network governance. Firms in Bangalore, the outsourcing hub in India, and firms in North America in places like the Silicon Valley show a high degree of interaction and interdependency that characterize network governance.

Social networks provide a useful conceptual lens to explore emergence of network governance across national boundaries. Strong social ties have been found to engender trust (Putnam 2000); however, Granovetter (1985) pointed out that strong social ties though instrumental in engendering trust are not very efficient in search for new information. The argument is simple but insightful as the information that circulates within strong ties is often redundant and fresh information is often acquired through weak ties. Thus, social networks perform two important but distinct functions – trust and search. As we have seen earlier, trust becomes even more important in the offshore outsourcing context due to institutional uncertainties. However, 'search' would equally have an important role to play as search for information about suitable partners across geographical space would be of paramount importance.

What role do networks play in the emergence of network governance across geographical spaces that are also temporally separated? What kinds of network ties facilitate both trust and search? The answer of these questions can perhaps provide a better explanation to the rise in offshore outsourcing rather than the narrowly conceived labour arbitrage argument generally provided.

Uncertainty has been typically conceptualized in a negative fashion in relation to the 'make or buy' decision. TCE holds that uncertainty of transaction costs is the main reason of firms organizing activities within hierarchy. Network governance literature emphasizes vertical de-aggregation in the presence of uncertainty, but only when there is a high degree of trust or structural embeddedness between the parties. Trust here is seen as an uncertainty reducing mechanism. But is uncertainty necessarily a bad thing?

DOI: 10.1057/9781137497321.0007

In financial markets for example, risk and reward go together. Literature on entrepreneurship emphasizes the way entrepreneurs embrace uncertainty and create value. In TCE, the governance mechanism is decided by assuming the transaction costs ex ante. Secondary proxies like asset specificity are used to estimate the transaction costs likely to be incurred which in turn determine the governance mechanism. However, actual transaction costs that a firm incurs ex post the decision are not taken into account. This is, as Beckert (1996) points out, the limitation of the rational actor model. One can be intentionally rational, as TCE suggests firms should be, by assuming secondary proxies like asset specificity to be reliable indicators of actual transaction costs.

As the governance choice is made ex ante, the difficulty is obvious in making a rational assertion that the governance mechanism chosen is the right one. This may happen in cases where, even in the presence of asset specificity, transaction costs turn out to be very low, meaning that firms might have lost out on opportunities to access the market mechanism. The understanding that uncertainty can cut both ways should make firms more circumspect in treating uncertainty in a one-dimensional fashion.

As mentioned earlier, in the outsourcing context, the decision to outsource is a 'make' and then 'buy' decision rather than 'make or buy' decision. The organizational history of making results in a set of capabilities, both tangible and intangible, gives strategic choices to the firm. One of the choices or 'real' options these capabilities offer is to allow firms to experiment more intensively with outsourcing. Uncertainty surrounding outsourcing can be mitigated not only by imposing sanctions, formal and informal, on external suppliers but also having strategic capabilities in-house. From the real option perspective, high uncertainty signals outsourcing opportunities to firms while in-house capabilities allow firms to take advantage of these opportunities.

In this research, it is acknowledged that uncertainty associated with outsourcing is multi-dimensional rather than the one-dimensional market uncertainty that has been usually discussed in the literature. Market uncertainty is combined with a set of internal uncertainties, which makes the outsourcing decision much more complex in nature.

While internal uncertainty is about how to deal with in-house capabilities that have been developed for the activities that are now to be outsourced and how to prioritize amongst various activities that are potential candidates for outsourcing, market uncertainty is about

DOI: 10.1057/9781137497321.0007

uncertainty about behaviour of potential exchange partners, and in the case of offshore outsourcing it is also about lack of knowledge about institutional setting in which potential exchange partners are embedded.

This research is about gaining an in-depth understanding of these various forms of uncertainties and also unpacking the various strategies that firms adopt to cope with these uncertainties.

2.2   Uncertainty and outsourcing

Chapter 1 contained a brief discussion of the various kinds of uncertainties that are specific to outsourcing. In this chapter, the discussion focuses around the issue of uncertainty related to economic action in general and outsourcing in particular. The different coping mechanisms that are adopted to cope with various forms of uncertainties are also discussed in depth. As we will see through the discussion, the choice of the coping mechanism is largely dependent on the context in which the uncertainty is felt by the involved actors.

There is a substantial body of literature that has looked at the issue of uncertainty in economic action and organizational responses to such uncertainty (Simon, 1957; Thomson, 1967; Podolny, 1994; Williamson, 1975). Uncertainty and trust are opposite sides of the same coin – existence of trust allows individuals, groups and organizations to overcome uncertainty and make economic action possible. Trust is deployed so pervasively in economic action that often it is done unconsciously (that is, people engage in economic action without consciously being aware that a lot of trust is being reposed on the other party). As Shapiro (1987) points out, many of the economic actions that are undertaken at individual, group or organizational level are not embedded in structures of personal relations. Social relations, she suggests are a sufficient condition but not a necessary condition for the existence of trust. Trust, which is not linked to social relations, can be defined as impersonal trust, and such trust is in reality a trust of the institutions – formal procedures, policing mechanisms, insurance arrangements and so on – which govern economic actions.

This view of course has resonance with North's (1990) idea of institutions as uncertainty reducing mechanisms. It has been suggested that institutions are the rules of the game formulated by social agents for social agents to reduce uncertainty in transactions, economic or otherwise (Hodgson, 2006; North, 1990). Though the idea of institutions encompasses both formal (for instance, laws, constitutions) and informal institutions (for instance, norms of behaviour, conventions and self-imposed codes of conduct), undoubtedly one of the main utilities of formal institutions is to reduce uncertainty and generate trust, albeit of an 'impersonal' nature.

So both trust and uncertainty are ubiquitous in human interactions, but the above discussion hints at the possibility that there are different forms of uncertainty and different forms of trust. This chapter is devoted to develop a better understanding of these forms of uncertainty and the coping mechanisms that are deployed to counter such uncertainties.

Uncertainty, as defined as the unpredictability of behaviour of agents to act in an opportunistic manner in any human interaction, can be managed mainly in two ways. First, uncertainty can be managed through social relations and through the trust it fosters (and punitive social sanctions in case there is a breach of trust). Second, uncertainty can be managed in an impersonal way by developing formal institutions like property laws and effective enforcing mechanisms. Of course, both approaches are not exclusive to each other. In most cases of economic action, parties employ a combination of inter-personal or inter-organizational trust that are aided by the presence of effective formal institutions that foster the kind of impersonal trust discussed before.

If one has to give examples of extreme cases where only one form of coping mechanism operates, one can cite the example of trade in a primitive society where there is an absence of formal institutions and economic exchange that takes place is embedded in a web of social relations and social sanctions. At the other end of the continuum an economic action that is characterized by a lack of personal relations and supported only by formal institutions would be a spot retail buying by a customer at a new supermarket chain. These two cases also depict the evolution of economic exchanges from the initial ones that were dominated by personal and social ties till the later ones characterized by impersonal exchanges. North (2005) cites the development of impersonal exchange as the key to market expansion witnessed from the eighteenth century onwards. North explains somewhat counter-intuitively that uncertainty and complexity of human interactions increased in parallel with reduction of uncertainty of the physical environment. Scientific progress in physical sciences has made the physical environment increasingly less uncertain and more predictable.

DOI: 10.1057/9781137497321.0007

However, taming of the physical environment has made a multitude of human interaction possible as never before, increasing both the uncertainty and complexity of such interactions. For example, progress in physical sciences has made international business an increasingly viable proposition and such scientific progress is dispersed across various industry sectors such as information technology, aerospace and shipbuilding. However, the physical possibility of international business has led to increased complexity of human interactions as long-distance trading often depends on impersonal exchanges and a different set of institutions had to evolve to cater for such exchanges (North, 1990).

The fact that many forms of economic exchanges are not linked to social relations and are based on impersonal trust underpinned by formal institutions does not mean that there are no market failures even in advanced Western societies. Information asymmetry between the seller and the buyer is central to the issue of uncertainty in an economic exchange. The seller typically knows more about the quality of the goods or services than the buyer. Akerlof (1970) showed that in cases of extreme information asymmetry, the market for a good and service will collapse as the market will consist of 'lemons', or poor quality product. Though market failures of this kind are relatively rare in developed nations, the information asymmetry between buyer and seller in varying degrees is a major contributor to the uncertainty of economic exchanges of all kinds. Lack of complete information available to actors challenges the rational actor model that has been one of the pillars of neo-classical economics. If actors do not possess the necessary information, how can they be sure that they maximize their utility ex post of the decision? Beckert (1996) characterizes this condition of actors as intentionally rational, that is, actors want to be rational yet they can be only be so in a limited sense. Of course this conception of actors is similar to Simon's (1991) idea of bounded rationality and Tversky and Kahneman's (1982) idea of heuristics. The main insight which emerges from the works of Tversky and Kahneman (1982) and Aronson (1991) on heuristics is that though the ubiquitous shortcuts that humans deploy in decision making in the absence of complete (or abundant but irrelevant) information are useful in coping with uncertainty but such decisions are also subject to systematic biases and use of heuristics has the inherent potentiality of suboptimal decisions being taken. The insight is important as uncertainty has been seen as one of the key determinants of establishing firm boundaries, and as in other forms of decision making, use of heuristics is also pervasive in firm, boundary-setting decisions (Simon, 1957).

DOI: 10.1057/9781137497321.0007

Uncertainty has been central to the explanation of why firms exist. Coase (1937) first talked about costs of accessing the market mechanism, which were later classified as transaction costs. According to Coase (1937), the cost of accessing the market to procure goods and services includes costs such as the cost of search for suitable partners, cost of monitoring a market relationship and cost of enforcement of contracts.

Coase posited that firms will internalize an activity within the boundaries of the firm when the internal cost of producing that activity is lower than the cost of procuring it from the market (which includes the nominal cost of the service plus the transaction costs associated with it). Williamson (1979) later introduced some behavioural assumptions to further develop the idea of transaction costs. Williamson argued that agents in an economic exchange will behave in an opportunistic fashion if there is incentive to do so. The incentive to cheat or behave opportunistically would arise if there are specific assets that have been invested by one of the party to make the economic exchange possible and if those assets do not have any alternate use. The asset specificity leads to uncertainty about transaction costs of a particular economic exchange and firms would tend to internalize activities with high asset specificity as the uncertainty associated with it would be too high. The behavioural assumptions made by Williamson have been challenged subsequently and such critiques have been discussed elsewhere in this research (Moran and Ghoshal, 1996; Granovetter, 1985). For the present purpose, it is sufficient to note that firms have been seen as entities that have evolved to cope with and reduce uncertainties in market transactions. It is also important to highlight the ubiquitous use of heuristics in decision making to cope with uncertainties that lead to establishment of firm boundaries.

In the following sections, the notion of uncertainty is further unpacked to understand the distinctiveness of uncertainty in the context of international business and in service exchanges. Also explored in some detail is the concept of 'Firm-Specific Uncertainty', though a more elaborated discussion on this is undertaken in Chapter 3.

2.3   Uncertainty in international business

An international business such as offshore outsourcing has its own uncertainties associated with it which have been found to be distinct to that associated with onshore transactions. Mascarenhas (1982) counts foreign exchange and political uncertainties as some of the uncertainties that businesses face when they go overseas, as does Miller (1992). It is useful to make the distinction between risk and uncertainty as it can be argued that uncertainties associated with foreign exchange fluctuations and political changes are better classified as risks than uncertainties. Knight (1921) suggested that risks are situations where a particular outcome can be assigned probabilities. In other words, risk is uncertainty that can be insured against, as the assignment of probabilities to different possible outcomes lies at the heart of insurance. Uncertainty on the other hand refers to situations where it is impossible to assign any probabilities to possible outcomes: uncertainties are uninsurable. Foreign exchange and interest rate fluctuations are more of a risk than uncertainty in this sense as it is mostly possible for firms to insure against these risks. Such risks certainly add to the overall cost of doing business but they can be estimated well in advance. In its internationalization strategy, a firm would consider such risks as a cost of doing business overseas and weigh them in relation with other potential advantages; for example, increased revenues or lower labour costs. Uncertainty is something which is uninsurable and thus is more of a cause for anxiety.

From North (1990) we know that institutions, both formal and informal, are coping mechanisms for uncertainties. Institutions impose constraints on behaviour thus making it more predictable. However, institutions are a social reality. They are constructed by human agents for human agents and exist only if there is collective acceptance of them in a particular community. Institutions are useful for predicting human behaviour only if one is aware of the rules of the game. For firms embarking on international business, it is the lack of knowledge of the institutions operating in the overseas location which is a major source of uncertainty. Formal institutions are always documented and thus can be easier to absorb, but this may not be the case always. Formal institutions interact with informal norms of behaviours in complex ways to create the rules of the game that make it harder for someone from overseas to grasp them easily. The word cultural barrier and differences is often used in international business, which can be a way of describing the faux pas often committed by firms operating in overseas locations.

There has been substantial empirical evidence that firms adopt a stage process in their internationalization strategy (Johanson and Valhne, 1977) by incrementally increasing their commitment to foreign markets. The strategy basically consists of gradually increasing knowledge of

DOI: 10.1057/9781137497321.0007

foreign markets by progressively making commitments, financial as well as psychological. The critical knowledge which is acquired would be the knowledge of local institutions both formal and informal.

There have of course been other empirical data that directly contradict the gradual stage process model. There are instances of 'born global' firms that have embarked on a full-fledged internationalization strategy right from the inception (Oviatt and Mcdougall, 1994). In the offshore outsourcing context, this phenomenon has been regularly observed in India where many of the Information Technology outsourcing firms fit the bill of 'born global'.

Both these strategies are possible in international business and the evidence of the stage model does not invalidate the 'born global' model or vice versa. Why this is so becomes clear as we understand how organizations try to cope with uncertainty in general and more specifically with uncertainty associated with international business. As has been mentioned, firms can use two generic strategies, often in combination, to cope with uncertainty. They can use trust engendered through social relations and impersonal trust engendered through a trust in institutions that govern transactions. And as some studies suggest, the case of 'born global' Information Technology outsourcing firms in India that have predominantly American customers can be explained through an investigation of the social ties of the founding members of such firms that reveals that the network ties of the entrepreneurs often have an American connection.

In other words, the social ties of the entrepreneurs often represent a form of social capital (Lin, 2001), the productive use of which is to reduce the uncertainty associated with international business. In the absence of strong social ties in an overseas country, firms can search for suitable partners but would normally seek out such partners in a country in whose formal institutions and enforcement of formal contracts the firm has reasons to repose faith. Thus, trust engendered through personal ties and efficient institutions and enforcement reduces transaction costs and helps firms in carrying out international business. It is important to note that the trust here is the 'initial' trust that is required for a transaction to fructify. Once there is a history of repeated transactions, the meeting of expectations of both the partners leads to the generation of more trust. This can launch the partnership into a virtuous cycle of trust where the partners are more inclined to take risks with each other (Huxham and Vaughan, 2001). Of course, if the initial expectations are not met

DOI: 10.1057/9781137497321.0007

satisfactorily, it can quickly lead to evaporation of trust, existence of social ties and efficient institutions notwithstanding.

The suggestion that repeated transactions lead to trust formation in international business has found empirical support (Gulati, 1995). From the discussion one can then suggest that uncertainty about human behaviour (firms do not behave opportunistically, it is people in the organizations that do) rises from the unobservable. Human intentionality is always unobservable as intentionality rises from consciousness which is unobservable (Searle, 1995). Social ties reduce the 'unobservable' problem in two ways. First, personal relations provide the opportunity to observe the behaviour of agents and from such an observation trust can arise. Additionally, ties that are embedded in a web of strong social relationships have the additional property of insurance against opportunistic behaviour through social sanctions. In the absence of social ties, institutions go a long way in fostering the initial trust in economic exchanges that take place across institutions.

If two firms that are embedded in different institutional structures hold a belief that the institutional framework within which the other is operating is efficient, that is, the rules of the game are fair and enforcement of contracts is possible, then this belief can lead to initial trust formation. Once the initial trust is formed, it is then possible to observe the behaviour of the other party, which forms the basis of more trust or distrust depending upon whether the initial expectations are met or not.

Thus, to conclude this part of the discussion, it can be said that in international business there is a duality of uncertainty. Uncertainty can arise from incomplete information on the behaviour of potential exchange partners and can also arise from lack of familiarity with institutions in which the exchange partners are embedded. It has been suggested that firms usually adopt two kinds of strategies to cope with this dual uncertainty. First, a firm can adopt an incremental strategy where it progressively reduces the uncertainty by increasing international exposure in a gradual fashion; second, it can use pre-existing social relations to cope with uncertainty and adopt a more aggressive, internationalization strategy.

2.4   Uncertainties in service transactions

It is suggested here that exchanges in service can be more uncertain than exchanges that are product based. Why this may be so is explained in the following section.

DOI: 10.1057/9781137497321.0007

It has earlier been mentioned that uncertainty in transaction costs has been cited as one of the main reasons why firms forgo market exchange and decide to produce within the firm (Coase, 1937). But what is meant by uncertainty of transaction costs? Transaction costs are the costs of accessing the market mechanism. These costs can be quite diverse, ranging from the cost of searching for a suitable trading partner, to the cost of finding out the quality of the goods and services on offer, to the cost of monitoring an exchange relationship, to the cost of enforcement of contract if required.

While some transaction costs are similar in nature for exchange relationships involving both goods and services, they differ in one important dimension: this is the cost associated with measurement of the quality of the goods and services on offer. There is certain information asymmetry involved in exchange relationships of all goods and services. The seller typically knows more about the quality of the goods and services on offer than the buyer. The buyer thus faces certain uncertainty with respect to the quality of goods on offer. It is suggested here that this uncertainty can be more severe in the case of service transactions relative to transactions that involve manufactured goods. Later in the section, the reason for this is explained but it is important to mention here that in an exchange the seller faces uncertainty too. When the transaction takes place in credit, there can be uncertainty of the buyer's creditworthiness, but the major source of uncertainty for the seller may come from the issue of asset specificity (Williamson, 1979). Asset specificity can arise if the seller has to invest in resources that would be specific to the exchange between the seller and a particular buyer, that is, that investment cannot be used to serve any other buyer that the seller may have. In other words, such investments would be specific to the exchange with no other alternate use. Williamson (1979) suggested that in such a condition the buyer may act opportunistically after the seller has invested into assets that have high specificity to the exchange. The buyer, knowing that the seller has no other productive use of the resource, can use that information as a leverage to negotiate lower price for himself. Thus, the condition of asset specificity can be a source of uncertainty for the seller especially when the asset specificity is very high. Williamson suggests that market exchange will not function efficiently in cases of high asset specificity and such transactions are likely to be organized within the hierarchy (firm) rather than be organized through the market.

DOI: 10.1057/9781137497321.0007

Coming back to the suggestion made earlier, why should the exercise of evaluating the quality of a service offering be more problematic than evaluating the quality of a product offering? North (1990) explains that when we buy a particular good or service, we are buying a host of attributes associated with the good or service. For example, the purchase of a house has different attributes associated with it, such as the quality of the structure, the environment of the neighbourhood and safety. To assess the value of the house, the buyer would need to measure the quality of different attributes separately and the difficulty of the task would depend on how easy it is to observe these attributes before buying. The less observable the attributes are to the buyer, the more uncertainty he faces about the quality, hence more effort (and more transaction costs incurred) required for the assessment of the same. One of the main distinctions between goods and services made is that while in goods the production and delivery of goods are separate processes, in services they are often the same (Lovelock, 1992). This can make the process of measurement of quality of the offering in services a more problematic endeavour relative to goods. Of course, there are exceptions to this rule. Some services like pre-packaged software are more like goods while some goods are dominated with pre- and after-sale services.

From the above discussion and the discussion preceding this section, it can be suggested that market uncertainty in offshore outsourcing of services can be seen at three levels. First, it can be said uncertainty in such exchanges can be behavioural, that is, potential exchange partners can act in opportunistic fashion and this can be a real source of uncertainty. Second, uncertainty can also be institutional, that is, as potential exchange partners are embedded in two different sets of institutions, there can be a lack of familiarity with each other's institutions leading to a heightened sense of uncertainty. Third, difficulty in measurement of service attributes can also lead to increased uncertainty. The heightened sense of uncertainty which firms often report in offshore outsourcing can thus be understood by taking these three levels of uncertainty into account.

2.5   Firm-specific uncertainty

Till now the discussion on uncertainty in outsourcing has focused around what can be termed market uncertainty, that is, the uncertainty that a firm encounters while trying to search for a potential exchange partner, assessing the suitability of the partner in provision of the service, and doing business in an institutional setting that can be alien to it. But firms also face a kind of uncertainty that is specific to each firm and arise out of the tacit nature of organizational networks (Krackhardt and Hanson, 1993) and organizational knowledge (Spender, 1996). The reason they are specific to the firm has to do with the path-dependent nature of organizational activities. Organization activities are performed through organizational routines and social network of intraorganizational actors. Such routines and social networks develop over time in a path-dependent fashion. Moreover as suggested by many (Krackardt, 1991; Burt, 2004; Freeman and Cameron, 1993), such networks are often informal and tacit. As pointed by Fisher and White (2000), reduction in firm size either through downsizing or through outsourcing or both, causes organizational restructuring that disrupts to varying degrees the embedded intraorganizational networks. The tacit nature of the network makes it difficult to predict ex ante the effect the restructuring will have on organizational performance. The literature on resource-based views of the firm (Barney, 1991; Hamel and Prahalad, 1990) emphasize that organizational knowledge is key to achieving competitive advantage in the marketplace. Spender (1996) has suggested that social and tacit knowledge is often the basis for a firm's competitive advantage. Nahapiet and Ghosal (1998) in similar vein have emphasized the role of social capital in production of critical organizational knowledge necessary for long-term sustainability of firms. The focus on organizational knowledge as the basis of both operational and strategic performance should make one circumspect of any restructuring activity that can affect organizational knowledge adversely. The firm-specific uncertainty arises from the unanticipated outcome of the outsourcing decision on the informal network of the organization. The firm-specific uncertainty and strategies to cope with such uncertainty are discussed in more detail in Chapter 4.

2.6   Multi-dimensional nature of uncertainty

From the above discussion, the multi-dimensional nature of uncertainty in outsourcing in general and more specifically in offshore outsourcing of service transactions becomes apparent. It can be said that the sources of uncertainty can be broadly classified into two categories – market uncertainty and firm-specific uncertainty. Under market uncertainty there

DOI: 10.1057/9781137497321.0007

can be three distinct sources. First, market uncertainty can be caused by incomplete information on behaviour of exchange partners. If there is no history of prior exchanges between trading partners, behavioural uncertainty can be a real concern especially if there are requirements to make relation-specific investments (asset specificity) by one of the exchange partners. Second, market uncertainty in the case of offshore outsourcing can also arise due to a lack of familiarity with institutions (both formal and informal) of exchange partners. The impersonal trust in local institutions that is often taken for granted by exchange partners co-located in the same institutional sphere can be found missing in offshore exchanges as in such cases partners have different sets of institutions and this can be a source of additional uncertainty. Third, in service outsourcing exchanges, uncertainty can be higher relative to manufactured good outsourcing owing to difficulty in measuring service attributes being exchanged. As all the three sources of market uncertainty can be present in offshore service exchanges, it then becomes comprehensible why such exchanges are generally considered more 'risky' than onshore outsourcing transactions.

Firm-specific uncertainty, on the other hand, can be present in all forms of outsourcing, be it onshore or offshore. Such uncertainty arises owing to the risk of loss of critical organizational knowledge due to the outsourcing process. Causal ambiguity between what is core and what is peripheral to organizational performance is the primary source of firm-specific uncertainty.

2.7   Strategies for coping with uncertainty

Though uncertainty in outsourcing is multi-dimensional, it is an empirical reality that firms manage to cope with such uncertainties as otherwise market transactions would not take place. Thus, it is important to understand the various coping mechanisms that firms deploy to counter uncertainty. The following section provides an overview of the discussion that is specified in more detail in Chapter 4.

As mentioned before, two generic strategies can be thought of for countering uncertainty. This is not a normative statement but more of a positive one. People have coped with uncertainty using these generic strategies as long as hominids have walked the earth. Personal and social ties obviously would have played a greater role in coping with uncertainty in the early part of the human evolution, when people cohabited in small groups. The trust engendered by social ties and the sanctions that the social structure imposes on opportunistic behaviour were the prime lubricants of the earlier economic exchanges (North, 1990). Reduction of physical uncertainties that came about with scientific progress in physical sciences allowed for long-distance trades, which necessitated new institutions to cope with the uncertainties of impersonal exchange. The source of 'initial' trust in impersonal exchanges does not derive from any social ties (as there aren't any by definition); rather it is derived from a belief that the institutions that support economic exchanges are fair and enforcement of contracts is possible. This does not mean that international business is predominantly a form of 'impersonal' exchange. International trade is often carried out through a complex web of social networks, and in reality, firms often use a combination of personal and social ties along with a belief in efficient institutions to embark on their internationalization strategy.

Saxenian (2002) coined the term 'transnational entrepreneurs'; an example of one such would be an entrepreneur who had been born and raised in India, went to the United States for higher education, worked extensively in multinational companies in the United States, thus building up an extensive personal and social network through his education and work. The entrepreneur then decides to come back and set up his own firm in India. For such an entrepreneur doing business in the United States (provided he has the right goods or services) would perhaps be a more natural choice than doing business in some obscure part of India, as he possesses a rich knowledge of different institutions in the United States along with many social ties representing the entrepreneur's (and the firm's) social capital.

While it is widely recognized that international business is generally more uncertain than business conducted locally, it is not often clear how firms cope with such uncertainties. Social capital of the firm and the entrepreneur is one such coping mechanism. Podolny (1994) argues that the greater the uncertainty, the more organizations engage in exchange relations with those whom they have transacted within the past. This is in conformity with the suggestion made earlier that repeated transactions build up trust which can launch partnerships into a virtuous cycle of increasing risk, meeting of expectations and increasing returns from the partnership. Podolny suggests that by adopting a strategy of selecting

DOI: 10.1057/9781137497321.0007

partners with whom the firms deals exclusively, it reduces the market uncertainty it faces.

This suggests that it is difficult for firms to assess the impact of outsourcing on organizational performance due to the collective and tacit nature of organizational knowledge. The role of intrafirm social capital that is vital in producing organizational knowledge (Burt, 2000) and organizational performance (Tsai and Ghoshal, 1998) is often underestimated in the context of outsourcing. The conscious outsourcing decision taken by individual agents often at the top of the hierarchy raises also the question of how aware these agents are of the informal networks that are operational through the organization. In Chapter 5, these issues are discussed in more detail and some strategies of countering the firm-specific uncertainty are offered.

2.8   Conclusion

In this chapter, the nature of the uncertainty in outsourcing has been discussed. What emerges out of the discussion is that such uncertainty is essentially multidimensional, consisting as it does of market and firm-specific uncertainty. While market uncertainty in outsourcing relates to the uncertainty in identification of suitable trading partners, difficulty in measurement of service attributes, unpredictability of behaviour of potential exchange partners and unfamiliarity of institutional setting of exchange partners, firm-specific uncertainty relates to the potential loss of intrafirm social capital due to outsourcing that may lead to the loss of competitive advantage and/or organizational performance.

Firms generally cope with uncertainty by having trust in the partners in an exchange or having trust in institutions that underpin impersonal exchanges or often in a combination of trust engendered partially through personal and social ties and efficient institutions. Personal and social ties as well as efficient institutions can be sources of initial trust, but once transactions take place, firms can observe the behaviour of others in an economic exchange, and depending upon whether expectations are met or not, trust is either reinforced or depreciated.

DOI: 10.1057/9781137497321.0007

In international business, use of trust generated through personal and social contacts has been empirically observed, and this evidence supports the suggestion that higher uncertainty necessitates higher trust. The exclusivity of partners and repeated transactions has been the specific strategies of some firms when operating under conditions of high uncertainty, as discussed earlier.

DOI: 10.1057/9781137497321.0007

3

Trust and Partnerships in Outsourcing

Datta, Surja and Neil Oschlag-Michael. *Understanding and Managing IT Outsourcing: A Partnership Approach.* Basingstoke: Palgrave Macmillan, 2015. DOI: 10.1057/9781137497321.0008.

DOI: 10.1057/9781137497321.0008

The aim in this section is to identify and understand various forms of trust and partnerships and explain how they are related and why trust can be conceptualized as partnerships.

3.1   Trust

That trust is rooted in relationships is well known: the first sentence used by the Oxford dictionary to explain trust is 'relations have to be built on trust'. While trust and the dictionary's initial definition of it, the 'firm belief in the reliability, truth, or ability of someone or something', is intangible, it is the subsequent definition that is of greater interest: the 'acceptance of the truth of a statement without evidence or investigation'. This definition is behaviour-specific, implies action and enables an assessment.

Golembiewski and McConkie (1975, cited in Bekmamedova et al., 2008) argue that it is difficult to conduct or compare trust research because of the widely divergent ways in which trust has been defined and measured. Given this complex and multi-faceted nature of trust, the literature reviewed in this chapter focuses on trust in the context of outsourcing and IT outsourcing in particular.

It is generally accepted that trust can emerge through different means (Gainey and Klaas, 2003), and there are suggestions of socially-oriented trust and cognitive-based trust being the two of them.

Socially oriented trust depends on each party adapting behaviour and acting in a reciprocal fashion, the aim being to be responsive to the other's needs. It evolves over time and is likely to lead to more stable, enduring relationships (Dorsch et al., 1998, cited in Gainey and Klaas, 2003). When trust develops, both parties believe that the other will look after their interests and behave responsibly because of a genuine concern for their welfare (Gainey and Klaas, 2003).

Cognitive-oriented trust relates to whether a party believes that the other side will conclude that it is in their best interest to behave responsibly. It is generally characterized by a short-term, almost suspicious approach where the supplier's performance is continually assessed (Lewicki, McAllister and Bies, 1998, cited in Gainey and Klaas, 2003). It emerges through rational calculation (Dasgupta, 1988, cited in Gainey and Klaas, 2003) and at the outset of a relationship one party generally examines the other party's incentives, reputation and past behaviour.

DOI: 10.1057/9781137497321.0008

Each might rationally conclude that the other party will behave responsibly and do as they promise.

While the relevance of cognitive-orientated trust is largely accepted within outsourcing, it is more difficult to argue for the relevance of socially oriented trust. However, cognitive-orientated trust is not the only classification of trust which is of relevance to IT outsourcing.

Trust orientations are not the only means of classifying trust, and there are other suggestions of how it can be classified, even within the context of outsourcing. Miranda and Kavan (2005), for instance, argue that there are two types: characteristic-based trust and process-based. Sabherwal (1999) argues that trust can be classified into four types: calculus-based, knowledge-based, identification-based and performance-based, the first three of which are based on an earlier classification suggested by Lewicki and Bunker (1996). The types discussed in the following subsections are based on Sabherwal (1999) and Lewicki and Bunker (1996) classifications.

Calculus-based is rooted in the rewards and punishments associated with a contract and the relationship is governed by structural controls and penalty clauses to minimize opportunistic behaviour. This trust implies monitoring and control and a high level of communication and is used to reduce the service receiver's risk, uncertainty or even fear. The rationale for the service provider is simple: increased business. Calculus-based trust is used interchangeably with deterrence-based trust (Rousseau et al., 1998, cited in Bekmamedova et. al., 2008). However, unlike calculus-based trust, which is based on a rational choice and is broader in scope, accounting both costs and benefits of violations, deterrence-based trust is relevant only for the costs of violations of trust (Paul and McDaniel 2004; Saparito et al. 2004; Shapiro et al. 1992, cited in Bekmamedova et. al., 2008).

Knowledge-based trust depends on the two parties knowing each other well and generally arises from shared experiences between the service provider and service receiver. It relies on information rather than deterrence and it develops over time, which allows them to develop a generalized expectancy that the other's behaviour is predictable and that they will act honourably (Lewicki and Bunker, 1996). While this form of trust can derive from key participants from the two parties knowing one another prior to the outsourcing relationship, it could also be facilitated by a 'courtship' whereby both parties seek to know each other well before starting the project (Sabherwal, 1999).

DOI: 10.1057/9781137497321.0008

Identification-based trust follows from the two parties identifying with each other's goals. Strong identification-based trust implies that both parties effectively understand and appreciate the other's needs and act towards delivering what is required. Trust is based on working towards shared goals and can be developed through early team building efforts and strengthened when personal goals are also taken into consideration. This type is similar to the character-based type suggested by Miranda and Kavan (2005) and is usually rooted in the expectation that parties with similar cultures have with each other.

Performance-based trust depends on the service outcome and level of success. Achieving goals improves cooperation and trust, whereas poor performance causes distrust. Celebrating successes jointly helps develop this trust even further. This form of trust underscores why the issue of trust is complex and its classification is difficult and arguably why Lewicki and Bunker (1996) never considered this type. Being strictly evidence-based, one could argue that this type does not imply trust at all and perhaps it is better classified as rhetorical trust, which is better explained by trust being used by two parties in a context where most external observers viewing it through an objective lens would not find justification for its existence.

3.2 Partnerships

Trust is best understood in the context of outsourcing partnerships and indeed one of the main observations of this study is that trust and partnerships can be used synonymously. This relationship and dependency between trust and partnerships is suggested in Leimeister and Krcmar's study in Oshri et al. (2008), which provides a list of partnership attributes which they refer to as relationship factors (refer to Table 3.1) and identifies trust as the attribute most associated with partnerships.

The low ranking of 'service quality' in their research is significant. It lends more evidence to the claim that performance-based trust is far less relevant to partnerships than knowledge-based trust and identification-based trust. The fact that performance-based trust is not aligned with the definition of trust, namely, the 'acceptance of the truth of a statement without evidence or investigation', provides far more conclusive evidence for this argument.

DOI: 10.1057/9781137497321.0008

TABLE 3.1   *Ranking of partnership attributes synthesized from the literature review*

Rank	Partnership attribute	Occurrences in literature review
1	Trust	20
2	Commitment	19
3	Communication	16
4	Conflict resolution	15
4	Dependency	15
6	Coordination	13
7	Balance of power	11
8	Culture similarity	10
9	Top-management support	8
10	Cooperation	7
10	Influence	7
12	Information sharing	6
13	Age of relationship	5
13	Consensus	5
13	Flexibility	5
16	Joint objectives	4
16	Reputation	4
18	Joint action	3
18	Norm development	3
20	Personal and social bonds	2
20	Service quality	2

Performance-based trust and calculus-based trust are well aligned with cognitive-oriented trust and none of them are characteristic of genuine partnerships. Performance-based trust only relates to service quality. High-service quality is not indicative of trust. While service quality is important in outsourcing relationships, it is at best a hygiene factor for partnerships; in the absence of sufficient service quality, relationships will not endure. However, partnerships don't exist simply because service quality is high. The same applies to calculus-based trust whose primary goal is to win a contract. This type of trust is better aligned with gaming than genuine partnerships.

Genuine partnerships (refer to Figure 3.1) are relationships with a high degree of identification-based trust and/or knowledge-based trust. These types of trust are also aligned with socially oriented trust.

That Information Technology outsourcing (ITO) partnerships matter is known, and studies conducted fifteen years ago have established partnership quality as a key predictor of outsourcing success (Lee and Kim, 1999). Other studies have shown that elements of partnership such as

DOI: 10.1057/9781137497321.0008

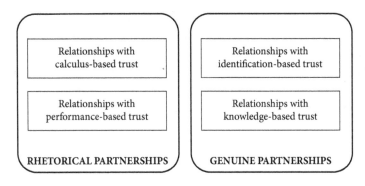

FIGURE 3.1   *Relationship between trust types and partnerships*
Source: Authors' own.

trust, cooperation and communication are important for success (Grover et al., 1996), and more recent studies have identified good relationships as being important for effective delivery and successful management (Willcocks et al., 2011).

Yet studies of outsourcing engagements also suggest that partnerships are rarely converted into practices and superior outcomes (Whitley and Willcocks, 2011) and they are not always pursued. This may be due to it being risky to depend more on relationships than on contracts to see work through (Willcocks and Lacity, 2009) and the assumption that one excludes the other, as certain partnership models suggest (Fitzgerald and Willcocks, 1994; Lee et al., 2003). Or the assumption that partnerships are not as relevant when TCE is the underlying rationale for outsourcing, which is often the case (Lacity et al., 2009).

There can be another explanation: partnerships are desirable yet difficult to operationalize. There is strong evidence for their being desirable among ITO practitioners. In an outsourcing survey conducted by Deloitte, a consultancy, 'a spirit of partnership between client and vendor' is identified as the factor which is most critical to successful outsourcing (Deloitte, 2012).

One of the challenges in pursuing partnerships is its intangible nature and the limited research on the characteristics of a partnership (Kern and Willcocks, 2000). Partnerships are difficult to identify and describe, let alone assess and quantify. Although partnership frameworks exist, they are constrained by the limitations of the underlying partnership 'schools' on which these frameworks are based. And they are constrained

DOI: 10.1057/9781137497321.0008

even further by the framework's not being operationalized. Without an operational partnership model it is difficult to analyze and assess a partnership, let alone define it.

At first glance it might appear to be easy to define what makes a true partnership, and Willcocks and Lacity (2009) suggest that outsourcing partnerships usually embody the following:

- ‘a non-reliance on the contract as the basis of the relationship
- a mutual desire to work things out, and a give-and-take philosophy
- a fair profit for the vendor, so that they do not seek to resort to what may be an inadequate contract
- the ability to work together in personal relationship terms
- the existence of a cultural fit between the client and vendor organizations
- good treatment of the client's transferred staff
- a perception that the vendor understands the client's business and problems’

However, despite the clarity of these statements, this is just one of several suggestions. In order to fully understand IT outsourcing partnerships, all perspectives need to be examined in detail.

These perspectives are synthesized by introducing the concept of partnership schools. A partnership school is any construct where there is a reference to an IT outsourcing partnership, whose characteristics distinguish it from general IT outsourcing business relationships. The notion of schools of partnership is inspired by Mintzberg et al.'s (1998) schools of strategy. Schools of partnership have common or similar goals, objectives or characteristics. What distinguishes them from each other is their underlying philosophy, focus and scope.

3.2.1   Partnership as a rhetoric

References to partnerships can be purely rhetorical, and research suggests that *strategic alliances exist more at the rhetorical* level than in practice (Willcocks and Lacity, 2009). The archetype of this perspective, however, is when it is used erroneously and when all relationships are referred to as partnerships or when vendors refer to themselves as partners by default. The weakness of this approach is self-evident. However, it is worth noting that perceptions do matter, and indeed there are

DOI: 10.1057/9781137497321.0008

arguments that the perceptions themselves are attributes of partnership (Lee and Kim, 2005).

This school of partnership is fully aligned with rhetoric-based trust.

3.2.2   Partnership as a contract

This school of partnership is based on the suggestion that partnerships cannot be divorced from the type of contract. Fitzgerald and Willcocks (1994) and Lee et al. (2003) focus on partnership from a contractual perspective, arguing that the notion of partnership cannot be divorced from the type of contract. Fitzgerald and Willcocks (1994) classify contracts into three types, one of which is a partnership, which they also refer to as a strategic alliance. They suggest that a partnership or strategic alliance is a collaborative relationship which involves the allocation of significant resources to maximize joint value. In contracts in these relationships, the partners agree to furnish a part of the capital and labour for a business enterprise, and each shares in profits and losses. Interestingly, this definition introduces another school of partnerships: that of strategic alliances, all of which are partnerships, in addition to those contracts which have partnership characteristics.

A weakness with this school is that *explaining the relationship between organizations via a purely contractual lens is unjustifiable because inter-organizational relationships can form from social learning and experiences* (Lee and Kim, 1999). The notion that there is more to strategic partnerships than contracts is also supported by Lacity and Rottman (2008), who suggest that partnerships become strategic by investing in the three dimensions of social capital: relational, cognitive and structural. Gulati (1995) also argues that partnerships do not rely only on a contract, that contracts and trust function as substitutes for each other and trust counteracts fears of opportunistic behaviour as satisfactorily as contracts do, and that contractual and non-contractual perspectives can be combined The purely contractual partnership has other limitations. Poppo and Zenger (2002) argue that contracts in themselves are unable to maintain the continuity of the relationship when unforeseen disturbances arise; and at the other end of this scale, Kishore et al. (2003) are not alone in arguing that the specifications for outsourced information services are difficult to specify completely a priori.

While certain partnership schools argue that there is little trust in purely contractual partnerships, trust is relevant when defined from a

Kern and Willcocks (2000) perspective, namely, the belief that a promise is reliable and will be fulfilled as stated in the contract. This school of partnership is fully aligned with knowledge-based trust, where the contract has strong partnership characteristics and to a lesser extent with identification-based trust. While the contract itself is also associated with calculus-based, its purpose in this context is completely different, namely on winning or awarding the contract and not the contractual characteristics themselves (which is where the spirit of partnership actually manifests itself).

3.2.3   Partnership as an alliance or strategic alliance

This perspective fits with the Fitzgerald and Willcocks (1994) definition of contractual partnerships The difference between the strategic alliance school and the contract school is that there is focus on far more than the contractual dimension and strategic dimension and it is generally accepted that shared strategic objectives are key to relationships becoming partnerships.

However, this is not always the case. Kishore et al. (2003), for instance, refer to strategic alliances merely as alliances and their model introduces the notion that there is more than just one type of strategic relationship. They argue partnerships can exist in non-strategic relationships.

Trust is an important attribute of this partnership school. Monitoring mechanisms are higher on trust than on contractual control, not least because the services involved are uncertain, dynamic and ambiguous (Kishore et al., 2003). Case studies suggest that flexibility, beyond the scope of what is defined in the contract, can only be achieved with trust (Fitzgerald and Willcocks, 1994). Strategic alliances and alliances are fully aligned with identification-based trust and alliances to a lesser extent with knowledge-based trust.

3.2.4   Partnership as a FORT type

This school of partnership is based on Kishore et al.'s (2003) four outsourcing relationship types (FORT) framework, which consists of two dimensions 'most germane to outsourcing relationships'. The first dimension focuses on the degree to which ownership and/or control have been transferred to service provider(s). The second dimension deals with the strategic impact of outsourced services.

DOI: 10.1057/9781137497321.0008

The types of IT outsourcing relationships in the framework are based on the degree of strategic impact and extent of substitution of ownership and/or control. Two of the four relationships in this framework, the alliance type and alignment type, are partnerships. They are called for when there is a high extent of substitution of ownership and/or control. An alliance type of outsourcing relationship is when there is high substitution of ownership and/or control and high strategic impact and an alignment type of outsourcing relationship is when there is high substitution of ownership and/or control and low strategic impact.

While the role of trust for the FORT alliance type is somewhat similar to the alliance school of partnership, it is called for as a means of 'creating a zipper to bind the client' (Kishore et al., 2003). Since the level of opportunism is less in the FORT alignment type, less trust is required in that type of relationship. As with alliances, this school of partnership is arguably best aligned with identification-based trust and knowledge-based trust although there are elements of calculus-based and deterrence-based trust since the underlying philosophy calls for making it difficult for 'partners' to leave a contract to pursue other substitutes in the market. Despite the similarities of FORT school and the strategic alliance school, they are different partnership perspective due to the assumptions underpinning the FORT framework.

3.2.5   Partnership as a relationship

The notion of a partnership relationship evolving from, and being opposed to, a contract relationship is a common one (Fitzgerald and Willcocks, 1994; McFarlan and Nolan, 1995; Grover et al., 1996; Lee et al., 2003). The weakness of this perspective, which defines partnership by the absence rather than the presence of certain contractual attributes or characteristics, is addressed by Oshri et al. (2008), who provide the inspiration for this school, where partnerships have a broader definition and are based on more than contractual types. Their notion of partnership allows for more than one type, and they suggest a comprehensive framework for describing outsourcing relationships along a variety of relationship dimensions. Their framework addresses weaknesses identified with other studies, such as being *'too one-sided'*. They suggest five types of IT outsourcing relationships, of which three types have partnership characteristics and two are called partnerships.

DOI: 10.1057/9781137497321.0008

One of these partnerships is a strategic alliance, which is similar to what is described in the alliance or strategic alliance school, namely a relationship characterized by sharing the risks and rewards, long-term engagement and high commitment. The other, a reliance partner, is when firms transfer IT operations to vendors for long periods without the relationship being a strategic alliance. The joint service development type of relationship, while not explicitly referred to as a partnership, has strong partnership characteristics and similarities with the 'partnership as an alliance' school. It is a type of relationship where 'parties develop selected outsourcing services together on a risk reward-basis using a behaviour-based governance form'.

While only the reliance-partner relationship calls for trust explicitly, implicit trust is an important attribute of all these relationships and all of them are associated with knowledge-based trust, the joint service development relationship and strategic alliance are best aligned with identification-based trust.

3.2.6   Partnership as evolution

In this school a partnership is perceived as proceeding along a learning or maturity curve. Willcocks et al. (2011) suggest a four-phase learning curve, from 'contract administration' through 'contract management' and 'supplier management' to 'collaborative innovation', the last of which is similar to their definition of a strategic partnership. Mehta and Mehta (2010) suggest a similar partnership maturity curve, with three phases ('outsourcing experimenters', 'outsourcing driven' and 'outsourcing centric') instead of four.

These suggestions are largely similar to Gottschalk and Solli-Sæther's (2006) evolutionary or 'stages of growth' model, which suggests that partnership is evolutionary. They suggest a three stage maturity model, which '*assume[s] that predictable patterns exist in the growth of organizations and in the growth of relationships among organizations*'. In this model the first stage is the cost stage and is well aligned with TCE. The second stage, the resource stage, is well aligned with RBV. The third and final stage is the partnership stage, which is 'based on partnership and alliance theory, relational exchange theory, stakeholder theory, and social exchange theory' (Gottschalk and Solli-Sæther, 2006).

This notion of evolution is also supported by Lasher et al. (1988, cited in Kern and Willcocks 2000). While time can and does influence partnerships, a weakness of this model is that it does not account for the possibility that, where desired, partnerships can exist from the outset and are not contingent on passing through other phases. Indeed, some models suggest that the notion of outsourcing maturity and partnership entails forming pre-project partnerships and that there is a targeted negotiation process before entering into a formal contract (Mehta and Mehta, 2010; Alexandrova, 2012), which most models consider to be the first stage.

Not all evolutionary approaches are linear and time dependent. Kishore et al. (2003) suggest a rather different approach with four types: alliance, support, alignment and reliance. Movement between the stages depends on the substitutability and strategic value of the services provided and not on time or maturity.

Trust is an important attribute in this school. Mehta and Mehta (2010) suggest building trust in a pre-project partnership especially to address frequently changing requirements. Willcocks et al.'s (2011) notion of collaboration is distinguished by high trust and Gottschalk and Solli-Sæther's (2006) notion of partnership emphasizes intangibles, such as trust. Kishore et al. (2003) suggest that trust rather than incentives and penalties becomes an important mechanism in alliance relationships, and Lee et al. (2003) emphasize that the relationship requires mutual trust rather than the sole pursuit of self-interest. While this partnership school is generally associated with identification-based trust in the final stage, it is arguably best associated with knowledge-based trust. In the initial stage success engenders performance-based trust, and elements of knowledge-based trust are introduced along the evolutionary journey. In the absence of success in the first stage of relationships, there is no possibility for performance-based trust arising and relationships cannot develop any further since they are most likely terminated.

3.2.7 Partnership as an outcome

This school of partnership is based on the intended outcome of an outsourcing relationship. While Lee et al. (2000) also suggest a two-stage evolutionary model, win-lose and win-win, their definition is based on the outcome and for them win-win is a partnership. This model is loosely similar to a two-stage evolution model, but its weakness is that it is biased, since it suggests that only partnerships result in win-win outcomes.

DOI: 10.1057/9781137497321.0008

Trust is cited as an attribute of this partnership school, which is similar to the partnership as evolution school. It is arguably best aligned with knowledge-based trust and to a lesser degree with identification-based trust in the win-win stage, although performance-based trust is a prerequisite for it to have progressed to the win-win stage.

3.2.8   Partnership as a purpose

This school is inspired by Kedia and Lahiri's (2007) suggestion that the nature of partnerships varies. They provide a *conceptual model that explains three types of IT outsourcing partnerships*: tactical, strategic and transformational. The tactical type of partnership is 'aimed at generating cost savings, preventing future investments or reducing staffing burden'. The strategic type of partnership is 'driven by need to remain locally responsive as well as be globally integrative, and the growing need to focus on core competences and develop capabilities'. The transformational type of partnership is characterized by 'rapid, step-change improvement in enterprise-level performance for the purpose of redefining existing businesses' (Kedia and Lahiri, 2007).

This school uses partnership as *a general term to mean cooperative behaviour between clients and providers* and to suggest that certain types of partnerships are aligned with TCE. This is consistent with suggestions that explaining relationships from a purely economic point of view is unjustifiable because inter-organizational relationships can form due to social interaction (Sun et al., 2002; Lee and Kim, 1999), which interestingly provides an explanation for why some partnership rhetoric may be justifiable.

Trust is very important in this school, and it is aligned with the RBV suggestion of it being considered a source of competitive advantage (Barney and Hansen, 1994, cited in Kedia and Lahiri 2007). The strategic and transformational types best aligned with identification-based trust and to a lesser extent with knowledge-based trust. The tactical type is best aligned with knowledge-based trust and to a limited extent with performance-based trust.

3.2.9   Partnership as a response

This school is inspired by Konsynski and McFarlan's (1990) suggestion that four types of partnerships emerge in response to the opportunities and ambience pressures that industries and companies face.

DOI: 10.1057/9781137497321.0008

Three of these four types of partnerships relate to service-provider and service-receiver relationships and are relevant for this study. The first type, a joint market partnership, calls for coordination with rivals where there is an advantage in order to specialize where specialization continues to make sense. The second type, an intra-industry partnership, is formed by small competitors who see an opportunity or a need to pool resources. The third type, a customer-supplier partnership, forms when 'information partnerships take off from data networks setup by suppliers to service customers'. The fourth and last type, an IT vendor-driven partnership, is 'based on partnership and alliance theory, relational exchange theory, stakeholder theory, and social exchange theory'.

While this school has similarities with the partnership as a purpose and partnership as an outcome schools, it differs in that it is sought purely as a response to external factors. Moreover, intangibles are of less relevance to this school than tangibles like clarity of the purpose and coordination, which is why these types are best aligned with identification-based trust and to a lesser extent with knowledge-based trust.

3.3   Conclusions

While some schools of partnerships are similar, others have little in common and some schools even appear to be mutually exclusive. However, there is one attribute which all schools of partnerships have in common: trust. This characteristic is used to suggest a new definition for outsourcing partnerships synthesized from the literature review (refer to Figure 3.2): genuine partnerships are relationships where there is a high degree of identification-based and/or knowledge-based trust.

Relationships based on a high degree of calculus-based and performance-based trust do not really focus on the spirit of trust or partnerships; they focus on firms awarding contracts to service providers with proven performance. These attributes are prerequisites for any outsourcing relationship to sustain itself and in their absence any relationship will most likely be terminated, however, their mere presence provides little, if any, evidence of a partnership. Moreover, as some scholars would argue, performance-based trust is not always a recognized type (Lewicki and Bunker, 1996).

DOI: 10.1057/9781137497321.0008

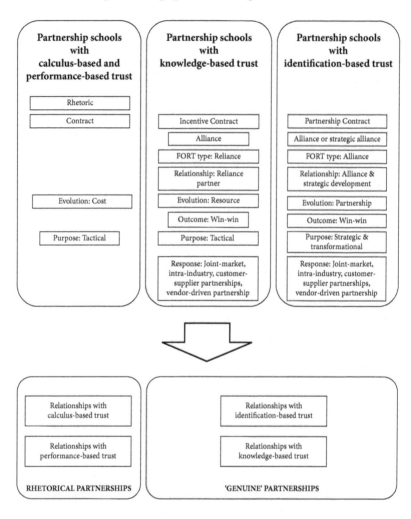

FIGURE 3.2   *Linking schools of partnership schools with types of trust*
Source: Authors' own.

DOI: 10.1057/9781137497321.0008

4

Developing Uncertainty and Trust Constructs

Datta, Surja and Neil Oschlag-Michael. *Understanding and Managing IT Outsourcing: A Partnership Approach.* Basingstoke: Palgrave Macmillan, 2015. DOI: 10.1057/9781137497321.0009.

▶

The purpose of this chapter is to develop a construct for uncertainty and trust. A three-step process is used to develop this construct. Initial constructs for uncertainty and trust are developed during the first two steps. These constructs are merged and reconciled in the third step to develop the final construct in which the relationship between trust and uncertainty is analyzed and reconciled.

4.1   Introduction

The assumptions underpinning the initial constructs are that uncertainty and trust can be identified or assessed through the attributes associated with them and that these attributes need to be synthesized from the literature review. If the attributes of uncertainty or trust are present, then there is uncertainty or trust and consequently if there are no attributes of uncertainty and trust then there is no uncertainty or trust present.

There are, however, a couple of issues associated with this assumption, and they need to be addressed by the construct: neither uncertainty nor trust is a binary issue and neither is simple. The issue that uncertainty and trust – and even their attributes – are not simple binary issues is addressed by considering them along a continuum where they are present to a low degree and gradually increase to where they are present to a high degree. The issue of simplicity is addressed by reducing the number of attributes to as few as possible and explaining them with the TCE and RBV theories (which have been discussed earlier).

4.2   Uncertainty

4.2.1   Uncertainty attributes and their sources

The categories for placing attributes in the construct emerge from the two main types of uncertainties identified in the literature review and their relationship with TCE and RBV theories. TCE posits that issues related to the market can be categorized into two types: search-related and transaction-related, of which transaction-related issues in turn can be categorized into enforce-related and control- and monitor-related issues. RBV focuses on the firm and the attributes selected are those related to the firm's competitiveness.

DOI: 10.1057/9781137497321.0009

TABLE 4.1   *Outsourcing uncertainty attributes and their sources*

Uncertainty attribute	Source
Impact on knowledge	Risk lists, Market uncertainty
Impact on flexibility	Risk lists
Future business environment	Risk lists
Future technology capability	Risk lists
Service quality	Risk lists
Infrastructure stability	Risk lists
Impact on reputation	Risk lists
Impact on innovation	Risk lists
Impact on competition position	Risk lists
Client perception	Risk lists
Impact on control	Risk lists
Level of information exchange	Market uncertainty
Level of institutional familiarity	Market uncertainty
Level of service measurement	Market uncertainty
Level of process opacity	Operational risk
Level of process codifiability	Operational risk
Relationship uncertainty	Structural risk

The uncertainty attributes (refer to Table 4.1) are synthesized from two main sources in the literature review:

1   Outsourcing risks: These uncertainty factors are synthesized from the consolidated risk lists and the operational and structural risks (identified in Chapter 1). The synthesis is based on the non-availability of insurance for these risks, the opportunity of them resulting in a better outcome than expected and the extent to which they can be mitigated with rigorous project management.
2   Market and firm uncertainties: These uncertainty factors are synthesized from market and firm-specific uncertainties (identified in Chapter 2).

Developing the uncertainty construct (refer to Figure 4.1) entails placing the main attributes from these sources within these categories. The resulting uncertainty construct has eight attributes:

▸ Service provider capabilities: whether the service provider has the ability to deliver the service
▸ Contract: whether the contract is codifiable ex ante and enforceable ex post
▸ Information exchange: whether the information required for control and transparency is available

DOI: 10.1057/9781137497321.0009

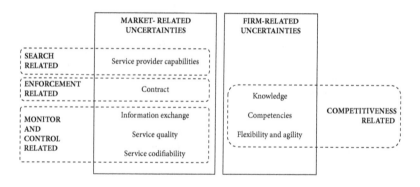

FIGURE 4.1   *Overview of main uncertainty attributes and their classification*
Source: Authors' own.

▶ Service quality: whether the service can be delivered at the required level
▶ Service codifiability: whether the service can be codified ex ante
▶ Knowledge: whether the firm can maintain and develop the knowledge resources (related to the outsourced service) it needs
▶ Competencies: whether the firm can maintain and develop the competencies to which the outsourced service relates
▶ Flexibility and agility: whether the firm can maintain the flexibility and agility it needs

4.2.2   Uncertainty attributes and their classification

There are four categories for these uncertainty attributes and they are best explained from the perspective of the categories to which they belong.

1   Search-related market uncertainties
2   Enforcement-related market uncertainties
3   Monitor- and control-related market uncertainties
4   Competitiveness-related firm uncertainties

Search-related market uncertainties manifest themselves in one main attribute: service provider capabilities. When firms search for outsourcing service providers they look for providers who have the capabilities to deliver the required service with which they can have a business relationship. Environmental-related uncertainties are excluded from the list of attributes as they manifest themselves in this attribute. For

DOI: 10.1057/9781137497321.0009

instance, if there is high uncertainty related to future technologies, then there will be high uncertainty related to the service provider's technology capabilities.

In situations where there is no uncertainty about service provider capabilities, there must be clarity on whether or not the service provider has the capabilities to deliver the service. If there is certainty that the service provider doesn't have the capabilities the service provider may not be selected, but this implies that there is no uncertainty related to the service itself and assumes that the capabilities cannot be developed. If there is certainty that the service provider has the capabilities and can deliver the service, it implies that there is no uncertainty related to the service itself. Therefore in certain situations the underlying service must be certain. In uncertain situations the capability may not be readily available with the service provider or the market, or the knowledge of the capability existing may not be readily available, in which case it may exist and even exceed service requirements.

Enforcement-related market uncertainties manifest themselves in one main attribute: the contract, with which there are several issues. Contractual uncertainty exists when the contract may be insufficient or when it may not be enforceable due to the legal environment, the relationship with the service provider, or prohibitive costs. If there is certainty that the contract is insufficient outsourcing may be avoided, but this also implies that there is no uncertainty related to the service itself and assumes that requirements are static, won't change and can be defined in the first place. If outsourcing is undertaken in uncertain situations, it is unlikely that the contract will receive much focus given its insufficiency, and it is likely that there is uncertainty related to the definition of requirements, which in turn is likely due to uncertainty related to the service itself.

Monitor- and control-related uncertainties manifest themselves in service- and information-related issues. The issue of service codifiability is one of the main uncertainty attributes and gives rise to many other uncertainties. At one end of the uncertainty continuum the service is a commodity or can be codified completely and there is no uncertainty because it can be measured, monitored and controlled. In this situation there is no uncertainty related to service requirements and service quality either and these can be defined completely and correctly ex ante. In this situation the service can be codified by the service provider and service levels and service quality can be – and often are – defined by the service

DOI: 10.1057/9781137497321.0009

provider ex ante. At the other end of the continuum, the service is not – or cannot be – codified which gives rise to uncertainty of whether the service can be delivered, let alone measured, monitored and controlled. In this situation there is also high uncertainty related to service requirements because these cannot be defined completely and correctly ex ante. Service transparency and the exchange of information need not be an issue when the service is a commodity; however, they assume much more importance when the service cannot be codified, especially when there is focus on control, because transparency is a prerequisite for measuring and monitoring, which in turn is highly dependent on the exchange of information between the parties. In uncertain situations the service will not be codifiable and the firm will not be able to define its information requirements correctly ex ante. Firms seeking to avoid uncertainty will not outsource services which are not codifiable due to the high uncertainty of control. However, in doing so they lose the opportunity to improve their control and transparency, if this is provided more efficiently by the market.

Firm uncertainties relate to the firm's competitiveness. While all of them could be covered with a single attribute, capabilities, it is more meaningful to list specific attributes to enable a more detailed examination. Knowledge and competencies related to the service outsourced

	LOW UNCERTAINTY ←	→ HIGH UNCERTAINTY
KNOWLEDGE (COMPET- ITIVENESS RELATED)	Knowledge exists and can be maintained	Knowledge may not be created or maintained OR knowledge may be created and maintained more efficiently
	Knowledge systems exist or do not need to change	Knowledge systems need to be developed OR are only available with the service provider
COMPETENCIES (COMPET- ITIVENESS RELATED)	Related competencies can be maintained and developed	Related competencies cannot be maintained and developed OR can be maintained and developed more efficiently
FLEXIBILITY AND AGILITY (COMPET- ITIVENESS RELATED)	No threat or influence on flexibility and agility	Flexibility and agility can get worse OR better

FIGURE 4.2   *Characteristics of firm-related attributes on the uncertainty continuum*
Source: Authors' own.

DOI: 10.1057/9781137497321.0009

	LOW UNCERTAINTY ←			→ HIGH UNCERTAINTY
SERVICE PROVIDER CAPABILITIES (SEARCH RELATED)	Capabilities are proven	Capabilities are known	Capabilities may exist	Capabilities don't exist and need to be developed OR exist and are unknown OR can be developed efficiently
	Reputation matters			Reputation is not a factor
	Several service providers have the capabilities			Only one service provider may have the capabilities
CONTRACT (ENFORCE RELATED)	Only contract required			Contract and relationship required
	Contract can be enforced easily			Contract cannot be enforced easily
	Requirements can be defined completely ex ante			Requirements can only be defined completely ex post
INFORMATION EXCHANGE (MONITOR & CONTROL RELATED)	High initial transparency			Low initial transparency
	Transparency and information level remain constant			Transparency decreases and information level falls OR transparency increases and information level rises
	All information is owned and accessible			Information is not owned and may not be accessible OR required information is not owned but may be accessible
SERVICE QUALITY (MONITOR & CONTROL RELATED)	Guarante of service quality			No guarantee of service quality
	Service quality remains constant			Service quality decreases OR increases
	Service quality is not dependent on contractual change management			Service quality is highly dependent on contractual change management
SERVICE CODIFIABILITY (MONITOR & CONTROL RELATED)	Commodity			Project delivered service
	Service is codifiable ex ante	Service may be codifiable		Service is not codifiable ex ante
	Infrastructure services	Application maintenance services		Application development and services integration projects

FIGURE 4.3 *Characteristics of market-related attributes on the uncertainty continuum*
Source: Authors' own.

lie at the heart of these uncertainties. In uncertain situations the firm cannot be certain that it will be able to develop, maintain and share the knowledge and competencies it requires to use or deliver the service and it may avoid outsourcing. However, in doing so it loses the opportunity to improve its knowledge and competencies, if this can be provided more

DOI: 10.1057/9781137497321.0009

efficiently by the market. Firm uncertainties also manifest themselves in agility and flexibility. Firms seeking to avoid uncertainty will not outsource services with uncertainty related to these attributes. However, in doing so they may lose the opportunity to improve or retain their competitiveness.

4.3   The two generic approaches to outsourcing

The uncertainty framework allows the elucidation of the two generic approaches to outsourcing. A firm can adopt an 'uncertainty avoidance' approach, an 'uncertainty embracing' one or a combination of the two.

Uncertainty avoidance: Under this approach a firm chooses to avoid all forms of market- and firm-specific uncertainty in its outsourcing relationships. The focus on avoidance of uncertainty greatly reduces the range of outsourcing opportunities but usually the payoff from a particular outsourcing relationship is much more certain as transaction costs can be calculated quite precisely before its commencement.

Uncertainty embracing: Here, as the name suggests, the firm adopts a more relaxed approach in relation to uncertainty in outsourcing relationships. The attitude stems from the realization that uncertainty signals both risk and reward. On the downside, market- and firm-specific uncertainties may translate into higher than expected costs of outsourcing but on the positive side, the payoff may be even greater than what was estimated at the commencement of the relationship. The range of outsourcing opportunities is greatly enhanced through this approach.

The hybrid: It is possible for firms to carefully combine the two approaches and develop a customized solution that caters to specific needs. For example, a firm may want to avoid market uncertainties while adopting a more relaxed approach in relation firm-specific uncertainties or vice versa.

4.4   Trust

4.4.1   Trust attributes and their sources

The approach taken to develop the trust construct is similar to the approach taken to develop the uncertainty construct. Initial trust attributes are synthesized from partnership attributes (refer to Table 3.1). These attributes are selected based on their importance and are then prioritized by the degree to which they relate with uncertainty attributes, resulting in the list below:

▶ Communication: whether communication reflects a spirit of trust and partnership
▶ Dependency: whether there is mutual dependency between both parties
▶ Conflict resolution: Whether conflicts are resolved in a spirit of trust and partnership
▶ Coordination: Whether coordination reflects a spirit of trust and partnership
▶ Balance of power: Whether the balance of power reflects a spirit of trust and partnership
▶ Culture: Whether cultural considerations reflect a spirit of trust and partnership
▶ Top management support: Whether top management are involved and their relationship reflects a spirit of trust and partnership
▶ Joint action: Whether both parties take joint action in a spirit of trust and partnership
▶ Information sharing: Whether information sharing reflects a spirit of trust and partnership
▶ Joint objectives: Whether both parties have joint objectives which reflect a spirit of trust and partnership
▶ Flexibility: Whether the flexibility exhibited by both parties reflects a spirit of trust and partnership
▶ Long-term focus: Whether relationships are old or decisions are made with the long term in mind
▶ Shared benefits: Whether the contract calls for sharing benefits realized in the relationship
▶ Cooperation: Whether cooperation reflects a spirit of trust and partnership
▶ Risk sharing: Whether the contract calls for sharing risk in the relationship.

4.4.2   Trust attributes and their classification

The trust attributes are classified within the same structure as the uncertainty construct:

1   Trust related to search-related market uncertainties
2   Trust related to enforcement-related market uncertainties

DOI: 10.1057/9781137497321.0009

3 Trust related to monitor- and control-related market uncertainties
4 Trust related to competitiveness-related firm uncertainties.

Trust related to search-related market uncertainties: Here trust relates to one main uncertainty attribute: service provider capabilities. When there is low trust, firms search for outsourcing service providers with existing capabilities. In the absence of knowledge of service providers, firms often consult with third parties whom they trust. The decision-making culture of the firm has a strong influence on the search and selection process. Reputable firms with quality products will most likely only choose reputable service providers with proven capabilities or with whom they have long-standing relationships. At the other end of the uncertainty continuum, in uncertain situations firms select service providers whom they deem fit, even if these don't have proven capabilities or prior knowledge of each other.

Calculus-based trust manifests itself best in situations where several service providers exist and there is certainty about their capability, since the contract can easily be used as an incentive (or threat) in this situation.

Identification-based trust manifests itself in situations where there is high uncertainty at the outset or where capabilities do not exist and need to be developed. It would be strongest in 'strategic partnership' or 'alliance' style relationships where trust associated with common goals and objectives is present from the outset. Trust in these relationships would have the effect of removing boundaries between the market and firm, thereby decreasing uncertainty.

Knowledge-based trust manifests itself in situations where there is high uncertainty at the outset. Here human interaction instils trust from the outset, despite the relationship not being a 'strategic partnership' or 'alliance'. Trust in these relationships would bring people from both parties closer together across boundaries between the market and firm, thereby decreasing uncertainty. Knowledge-based trust also plays a strong role in 'strategic partnership' or 'alliance' style relationships, because there needs to be a great degree of trust, with corresponding close human relationships between key negotiators and decision makers for such outsourcing relationships to arise.

Performance-based trust does not manifest itself in situations where there are any search-related uncertainties, as it only exists when there is certainty that the service can be delivered and the capabilities are readily available.

Trust related to enforcement-related market uncertainties: Here trust is associated with one main issue: the contract. On one end of the continuum, trust is not relevant as there is no uncertainty related to enforcing the contract. In these situations there is no uncertainty related to the requirements which can be defined ex ante. Contracts in these relationships are typically fixed price and have no partnership characteristics. At the other end of the continuum, there is high contractual uncertainty and requirements and responsibilities cannot be defined ex ante. Here trust manifests itself strongly in 'joint objectives', 'benefit sharing' and 'risk sharing' attributes, all of which are related to the contract. Contracts in these relationships have strong partnership characteristics. The decision-making culture of the firm has a strong influence on the enforcement uncertainty it will accept. Firms which place strong emphasis on control will outsource only when they are certain that the contract can be enforced. At the other end of the uncertainty continuum, in uncertain situations, firms place far less emphasis on the contract and will often resolve disputes based on joint objectives rather than requirements, without referring to the contract or resorting to contractual measures.

While calculus-based trust is strongly associated with the contract and appears to be related to enforcement-related uncertainty, this is not the case. It is associated only with uncertainty related to awarding the contract which is actually a search-related uncertainty. It does not manifest itself in situations where there are any enforcement-related uncertainties, as the contract is terminated in these situations. It exists only when there is certainty that the service can be delivered by more than one service provider, implying that service levels can be defined in the contract ex ante along with all requirements.

Identification-based trust manifests itself strongly in situations where there is high contractual uncertainty. Trust manifests itself in 'joint objectives', 'benefit sharing', 'risk sharing' attributes, all of which are related to the contract. Contracts in these relationships would typically have strong partnership characteristics with benefit and risk sharing. It would be strongest in 'strategic partnership' or 'alliance' style relationships where common goals and objectives provide direction, since requirements cannot be defined ex ante. Trust in these relationships would have the effect of simply sharing the uncertainty that exists.

Knowledge-based trust manifests itself to a lesser degree than identification-based trust. Contracts in these relationships would typically be incentivized to align objectives and disputes are more likely to be settled based on common goals and relationships than the contract alone.

DOI: 10.1057/9781137497321.0009

Performance-based trust does not manifest itself in situations where there are any enforcement-related uncertainties, as it exists only when there is certainty that the service can be delivered, implying that service levels can be defined in the contract ex ante along with all requirements.

Trust related to monitor- and control-related market uncertainties: Both trust and uncertainty manifest themselves in more than one attribute. There is a strong correlation between the uncertainty attribute, 'information exchange' and the trust attributes 'communication' and 'information sharing'. On one end of the continuum trust is not relevant as there is no uncertainty related to exchanging information. This could be due to high existing transparency, automation of information systems or because the information related to the outsourced service is of little importance. Communication and information sharing in this situation would likely reflect little more than is reflected in the contract. In these situations there is no uncertainty related to information requirements which can be defined ex ante. At the other end of the continuum, information is of more importance and there is less automation and transparency. Here trust manifests itself strongly in 'communication' and 'information sharing' attributes. There is stronger communication with more human involvement and much more information and knowledge is shared proactively. Information will more likely be available on demand than according to contractual requirements. The control culture of the firm has a strong influence on the control uncertainty it will accept. Firms which place strong emphasis on control will only outsource when they are certain that the information required for control is available.

Similarly 'service quality' and 'codifiability' are certain at one end of the monitor- and control-related continuum and trust is not required (although performance-based trust exists). This would be typical for situations where the services outsourced are commodities or completely codifiable or where warranties and guarantees exist and where change management is not an issue. Firms which place strong emphasis on control will outsource services only when they are codifiable. They are more likely to outsource infrastructure services than system integration projects. At the other end of the continuum the service is not codifiable and there is uncertainty regarding its quality. Uncertainty related to codifiability lies at the heart of all market uncertainty. Since the service requirements cannot be defined ex ante in these situations, significant change management, control and oversight are required, as a result of which trust assumes great importance.

Calculus-based trust is not associated with these uncertainties. It exists only when there is certainty that the contract can be transferred from one to another service provider, implying that there is little uncertainty related to the service itself and that requirement can be defined ex ante.

Identification-based trust manifests itself strongly in 'communication' and 'information sharing' attributes in uncertain situations, not least because the need for strong communication and information sharing increases in uncertain situations where information requirements cannot be codified ex ante. Information sharing is more likely to be proactive and on demand with emphasis on face-to-face meetings and co-location to improve communication.

Knowledge-based trust also manifests itself strongly in 'communication' and 'information sharing' attributes. The importance of human interaction in these relations will emphasize face-to-face meetings and co-location.

Performance-based trust does not manifest itself in situations where there are any monitor- and control-related uncertainties, as it exists only when there is certainty that the service can be monitored, controlled and delivered, implying that service levels can be defined in the contract ex ante along with all requirements.

Trust related to competitiveness-related firm uncertainties: Both trust and uncertainty manifest themselves in more than one attribute. There is a strong correlation between the uncertainty attributes 'knowledge' and 'competencies' and the trust attributes 'communication' and 'knowledge sharing'. On one end of the continuum, trust is not relevant as there is no uncertainty related to losing knowledge or competencies and knowledge sharing is less important. At the other end of the continuum, knowledge can be gained or lost and competencies could develop or be eroded. Here trust manifests itself strongly in 'communication' and 'knowledge sharing' attributes. The control culture of the firm has a strong influence on the control uncertainty it will accept. Firms which place strong emphasis on knowledge will outsource only when they are certain that the knowledge they require is owned and available in uncertain situations and they are likely to insist on strong service provider knowledge management systems. At the other end of the continuum, firms that outsource in uncertain situations need trust, which will manifest itself in sharing data, knowledge and systems with the aim of developing their capabilities and improving their competitiveness.

Firms which seek to avoid uncertain situations will not outsource services when there is uncertainty related to their organizational flexibility

DOI: 10.1057/9781137497321.0009

and agility due to the risk of some form of dependency. At the other end of the continuum, firms outsource services when there is uncertainty related to their flexibility, and trust manifests itself by them becoming mutually dependant on each other.

Identification-based trust manifests itself strongly in 'communication' and 'knowledge sharing' attributes in uncertain situations, not least because of the importance of knowledge sharing in building capabilities, which can be an objective of the outsourcing relationship. It also manifests itself in mutual dependency between both parties and is an inherent characteristic of strategic alliances partnerships.

Knowledge-based trust manifests itself strongly in the 'knowledge sharing' attribute. The importance of human interaction in these relations will emphasize face-to-face meetings and co-location. Calculus-based and performance-based trust are not associated with these uncertainties. Knowledge-based trust will allow dependency as long as it is mutually beneficial, even if it is not within a strategic alliance style relationship.

The characteristics of these trust attributes can also be illustrated along the uncertainty continuum (refer to Figures 4.4 and 4.5).

	UNCERTAINTY AVOIDING ← RELATIONSHIPS	→ UNCERTAINTY EMBRACING RELATIONSHIPS
SERVICE CODIFIABILITY (MONITOR & CONTROL RELATED)	Outsource when there is high transparency and complete control	Outsource even when there is low transparency and only joint control
	Outsource when service is a commodity or codifiable ex ante	Outsource even when service is not codifiable ex ante
KNOWLEDGE AND COMPETENCIES (COMPET-ITIVENESS RELATED)	Outsource when there is no risk of losing knowledge	Outsource to develop or maintain knowledge
	Exchange data and information	Exchange data, information and knowledge
	Focus on maintaining or improving service quality	Focus on maintaining or improving service quality and underlying competencies
	Own data and knowledge	Share data and knowledge
FLEXIBILITY AND AGILITY (COMPET-ITIVENESS RELATED)	Outsource when there is no dependency	Outsource even when there is dependency
	Outsource if there is no risk of losing agility and flexibility	Outsource to improve agility and flexibility

FIGURE 4.4   *Characteristics of trust attributes in outsourcing relationships*
Source: Authors' own.

DOI: 10.1057/9781137497321.0009

	UNCERTAINTY AVOIDING ← RELATIONSHIPS	→ UNCERTAINTY EMBRACING RELATIONSHIPS
SERVICE PROVIDER CAPABILITIES (SEARCH RELATED)	Outsource only when several service providers have proven capabilities Trust large reputable service providers	Outsource even when service provider and service receiver need to develop capabilities jointly Trust small or unknown service providers
CONTRACT (ENFORCE RELATED)	Trust the contract and use it to settle disputes Outsource when requirements can be defined ex ante Draw a fixed price contract and do not share benefits or risks Focus on requirements and service quality	Trust the relationship and use long-term objectives to settle disputes Outsource even when requirements can only be defined ex post Draw a partnership contract and share benefits and risks Focus on service quality and joint objectives
INFORMATION EXCHANGE (MONITOR & CONTROL RELATED)	Outsource when there is high transparency and control Exchange data and information Only exchange information which one is contractually obliged to Rely on systems Use tools like screen sharing to improve communication Top management is involved Coordination and cooperation	Outsource even when there is low transparency and only joint control Exchange data, information and knowledge Exchange information even when one is not contractually obliged to Rely on people Use tools, face-to-face meetings and co-location to improve communication Top management is involved but decisions can also be made at lower levels Joint decision making, joint planning and joint action
SERVICE QUALITY (MONITOR & CONTROL RELATED)	Trust depends on guarantees or warranties Coordination and joint planning Little change and no change without formal change management	Trust depends on relationships and joint objectives Joint planning, joint action and joint decision making Significant change and change occurs even without formal change management

FIGURE 4.5 *Characteristics of trust attributes in outsourcing relationships*
Source: Authors' own.

DOI: 10.1057/9781137497321.0009

4.5   Linking trust and uncertainty

The construct explains the relationship between trust and uncertainty (refer to Figure 4.6) and explains how trust types manifest themselves in uncertain situations.

Performance-based trust is the only trust type which is not associated with uncertainty. While it is strongly associated with the 'service quality' attribute, it has to be earned and exists only when there is certainty that service quality is high. This finding supports the argument that performance-based trust is a weak trust type. Alternately, it is an example of rhetorical trust at its very best.

While calculus-based trust is strongly associated with the 'contract' attribute, it actually only manifests itself when there is uncertainty about awarding the contract and it is related to search uncertainty. It is present – and may exist only – in the pre-award phases of the contract, where there is uncertainty about whom the contract should be awarded to. Once the contract is awarded it does not manifest itself until the contract is due for extension (or termination). It needs to be underscored that contractual uncertainty in this relationship is limited to one small aspect: the contract award. The contract itself has no trust or uncertainty attributes and that the relationship is aligned with rhetorical trust, which assumes that a partnership exists simply because a contract has been awarded.

Knowledge-based trust is associated with all the uncertainty attributes. However, it is not strongly associated with 'service quality' uncertainty, which is an implicit requirement for the outsourcing relationship to

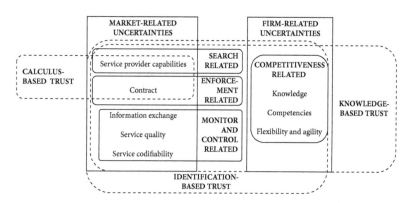

FIGURE 4.6   *Overview of the relationship between trust and uncertainty types*
Source: Authors' own.

DOI: 10.1057/9781137497321.0009

continue in the long term. Knowledge-based trust relationships value knowledge and communication and place strong emphasis on human interaction. It differs significantly with calculus-based trust and performance-based trust in that it manifests itself in many more trust attributes.

Identification-based trust is strongly associated with all uncertainty attributes. While it has similar attributes to knowledge-based trust, it differs to the degree to which trust is manifested in them. It differs from calculus-based trust in that there is no uncertainty about the 'contract award', and it is typical of strategic alliances partnerships where joint objectives and partnership style contracts exist from the outset. It can exist at the outset despite there being 'service quality' uncertainty; however, this is an implicit requirement for the outsourcing relationship to continue in the long term.

4.6 Conclusions

The conceptual framework developed in this chapter has integrated the two distinct but related themes of uncertainty and trust. It has specified the forms of trust that are most adept at coping with uncertainty – be it market-specific or firm-specific in nature. The framework is the theoretical lens through which the paradigmatic case studies that are documented in the next chapter are explored.

DOI: 10.1057/9781137497321.0009

5

Findings and Discussion on Case Studies

Datta, Surja and Neil Oschlag-Michael. *Understanding and Managing IT Outsourcing: A Partnership Approach*. Basingstoke: Palgrave Macmillan, 2015. DOI: 10.1057/9781137497321.0010.

▶

DOI: 10.1057/9781137497321.0010

5.1   Introduction

The main purpose of the case studies is to examine how trust and uncertainty are related and how they can be understood with the constructs developed in Chapter 4. Our concern is not with 'validation' of the frameworks but rather with the task of demonstrating how these theoretical constructs work in practice. A secondary objective is to develop an idea of how trust can be engendered over time between service providers and service receivers in outsourcing relationships that may have high uncertainty associated with them at least in the initial stages.

5.2   Case study – Alpha

Alpha is a global FMCG firm with premium global brands and thousands of employees. The case-study participant is Alpha's Application Services Director.

5.2.1   Background and context

Alpha was founded scores of years ago when it sold a single product in one country. With time it has grown through mergers and acquisitions and it is now a leading firm within its sector. For most of its history its acquisitions were run relatively independently. That changed in 2000 and the firm is now in the process of being consolidated globally from a business and IT perspective. While IT is still a support function, it is critical, increasingly complex and an integral component of all business processes.

5.2.2   Infrastructure services

Alpha's globalization journey started in 2000, with a consolidation in its main region. This consolidation included back-office functions and introduced the notion of a common global strategy and common policies. The IT outsourcing journey started slightly later and the notion of shared infrastructure, solution and organization was introduced following feasibility studies conducted in IT and finance.

The feasibility studies were followed by a consolidation, which called for a shared Enterprise Resource Planning (ERP) system and shared organization a few years later. The main drivers of the case underlying the

DOI: 10.1057/9781137497321.0010

consolidation were to increase financial transparency and efficiency. The finance functions were set up in a near-shore captive centre and initial scope included simple processes like accounts payable and accounts receivable. Gradually, scope was increased to include more complex processes and in 2004 a decision was taken to extend the shared organization from the few countries in the main region to the entire region.

IT outsourcing started with infrastructure, which was where the consolidation had begun. One of the drivers for outsourcing was that the company did not have the time or resources for the transformation underpinning the consolidation. Alpha initiated discussions with three outsourcing companies. By this time it had already conducted an analysis and developed a plan for its infrastructure The selection criteria for the service provider was based on their alignment with this plan, the savings it envisaged and their ability to present a solution which caused as little disruption as possible to ongoing operations functions during the process.

One of the goals of the transformation was to outsource infrastructure services and consolidate solutions across the entire region. In 2007 these services were transitioned to the service provider for a period of seven years. This contract was an outcome-based one and there was no focus on any infrastructure service components, like data centres. However, there were issues with this approach and the service provider was later replaced. This decision was driven by the desire for a new operating model to reduce the loss of flexibility and control and to avoid the risk of lock-in with service providers.

The original operating model allowed the service provider to control all infrastructure service components. The current model is based on a separation of infrastructure solution components including hardware, network and services. This separation means that there is no longer any uncertainty associated with the contract as Alpha has complete control of its own infrastructure and the flexibility to reconfigure components.

The commitment and buy-in from the current service provider was a key reason for the selection. When the infrastructure services were transitioned to it, the delivery model was transformed and only the service component was transitioned from the former service provider. Components like hardware, inventory and data centres were insourced during the process and are now managed internally.

DOI: 10.1057/9781137497321.0010

This separation removed an undesired dependency and makes it much easier to transition services from one service provider to another and implement multi-sourcing models. This model provides motivation for service providers to continuously provide high service quality given the ease with which the service they provide can be transitioned to other service providers.

However, the model raises new issues related to Alpha's service provider management capabilities as more service providers are involved. Issues like controlling SLAs or measuring performance, which used to be relatively straightforward, are far more complex now and this is only compounded by the underlying complexity and scope of the services.

The consolidation has been successful and now there are plans to extend scope to include other business regions. The model in these regions will be similar to the existing one in the main region, with the service being separated into components to maintain control and avoid any dependency.

5.2.3   Application services

When the consolidation with Alpha's infrastructure services began, its ERP applications and systems operated in their own country-based silos. A couple of years later this was consolidated and rolled out one country at a time on a shared platform in its region. This consolidation is nearly complete. Although another service provider participates in this initiative, Alpha does not consider this outsourcing in the classical sense, as it is controlled completely by its internal IT function. This consolidation has had a lot of dependencies with underlying business processes and also resulted in process and structure standardization in this region. The drivers of the case underlying this consolidation were the need for greater transparency, a common overview and reporting to support it. From a business perspective, this IT consolidation is coordinated with other related initiatives, including building a shared supply chain.

The need for application maintenance services arose in 2010. Once new applications were rolled out they needed to be maintained. The contract for application maintenance was awarded to the service provider, who was responsible for application development, which is based on an offshore delivery model. By this stage, ten years after the outsourcing journey had begun, offshore outsourcing was no longer considered uncertain, given that many applications were being rolled out in foreign countries anyway. It was deemed beneficial to include the maintenance of the legacy systems, which are being replaced by the new ones in this contract. This contract is successful and was renewed recently.

Given the satisfaction with application maintenance and infrastructure delivery, a shared model is being considered for application development outsourcing. Interestingly, it is at this stage that the term 'partner' is first used ('The contract we have with our partner is for managed delivery service and the partner has a high level of responsibility in the program'). With time this delivery model has evolved to an on-site-offshore one from a purely on-site-based one. There is no uncertainty associated with offshoring as the company's own application development team has grown accustomed to working with the service provider's on-site and offshore team during the ERP implementation program.

5.2.4   Analysis of trust and uncertainty

Alpha's outsourcing strategy is influenced by trust and uncertainty and there is virtually no uncertainty and very little trust in the relationship. In the absence of trust, there is a deliberate decision to avoid any uncertainty. This is partly due to the culture of the firm and partly due to the performance and behaviour of service providers. There is very little uncertainty in Alpha's outsourcing relationships as a result of which the relationship is characterized mostly by performance-based trust. Although it is aligned with rhetoric-based trust and elements of calculus-based and even knowledge-based trust are present to a limited extent, it is not a partnership.

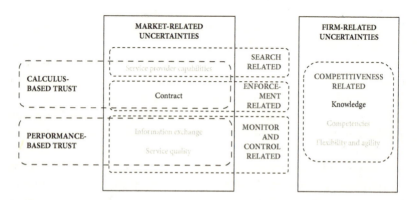

FIGURE 5.1   *Relationship between uncertainty attributes and trust types*
Source: Authors' own.

DOI: 10.1057/9781137497321.0010

There are no search-related uncertainties as the service providers considered are renowned, reputable and vetted by third parties and have proven capabilities. There is no uncertainty related to existing service provider capabilities or relationships, which are regarded only as contractual ones. Given Alpha's culture the most important factors in assessing service providers is the quality of their solutions, their underlying capability and their reputation. It would be unthinkable to select a service provider based on personal relationships or trust alone. Alpha's culture and its focus on quality and control to support its premium products and brand make it reduce any market uncertainty related to control and service quality, as a result of which there is virtually no uncertainty related to control.

There is a correlation between this situation and the calculus-based trust used to motivate service providers: in the absence of sufficient control and quality, contracts will be terminated and services can be transitioned between service providers with ease. If there is high control and service quality, as is the case, there is performance-based trust in the relationship and contracts will be extended. Both of these measures have been applied successfully.

Since there is a conscious decision to reduce uncertainty and dependency and maintain as much control as possible and uncertainty cannot be avoided, it influences outsourcing strategy. This decision essentially focuses on outsourcing services, which are codifiable and controllable. Given the absence of trust and the decision to avoid dependency there is justifiable concern about the uncertainty of losing knowledge and competencies related to the services outsourced, especially in the future when outsourcing will likely be extended to 'buy' as opposed to the 'make and then buy' approach used currently.

On being asked to comment on the use of the term 'partner', it is confirmed that it is used only in the partnership in a rhetorical sense. The explanation offered is that there is no such thing as a partnership unless it is joint venture or based on a joint investment. Outsourcing relationships are business relationships where each part has different goals and needs. There is a suggestion that trust helps but that it should be earned through performance and be reflected in investments by the service provider, something for which there is no evidence. Knowledge-based trust exists in a weak form, which is typical of certain situations, but there is an acknowledgement that it could develop further with time, and focus is on performance-based trust, in keeping with company culture.

DOI: 10.1057/9781137497321.0010

This case is not uncommon and illustrates how firms manage uncertainty. When there is low uncertainty there is no need for trust, and when there is low trust, uncertainty is avoided. This decision is economically sound. Outsourcing scope is determined by identifying services with low uncertainty, essentially limiting it to codifiable and transparent services, for which there is a high level of control. The downside of this approach is that all available services in the market – and the benefits associated with them – are not exploited completely.

5.3   Case study – Beta

Beta is an international management consultancy with hundreds of employees. The case study participants are the IT Manager and a management consultant who is an IT system owner and also manages the outsourcing contract and relationship.

5.3.1   Background and context

Beta is a management consultancy whose business model is based on the quality of its consultants, its relationships with its clients and the business outcomes of its engagements with them. While Beta has a client-facing IT management practice, the IT function itself is a small support function, yet crucial for operations and delivery.

When Beta was founded its initial IT infrastructure setup had more in common with what one finds in ordinary homes nowadays, augmented with a few ERP applications. Gradually complexity increased and IT systems grew to include more applications and a portal.

5.3.2   Infrastructure services

Infrastructure outsourcing was first considered in 2006, shortly after which some infrastructure services and support functions were outsourced. These services were transitioned to the current service provider about four years ago due to performance-related issues with the original service provider. The main outsourcing driver at that stage was the need to have 24–7 support for Beta's growing team of consultants. By this stage Beta had internationalized and established offices in other countries. The IT function had increasing difficulty providing operations support, which often entailed driving to the office outside normal

DOI: 10.1057/9781137497321.0010

working hours to reboot a server or perform other routine tasks, many of which were becoming increasingly complex. Service level and price were key factors in selecting the current infrastructure service provider. Global outsourcing service providers were not considered due to the expectation of incompatible work cultures and the down-prioritization of Beta's small contract.

The infrastructure services outsourced are simple and can be codified and there is virtually no uncertainty associated with them. While there is an expectation and realization of high service levels at competitive pricing, there is also an excellent working relationship with the service provider. However, services like these are commodities, and a contractual extension is not contingent on anything other than high service levels and competitive pricing.

5.3.3 Application services

These services are far more relevant for this study. Beta's portal development and maintenance functions were outsourced four years ago, and there was very high uncertainty associated with its requirements and objectives and service provider capabilities at the outset.

Beta's infrastructure provider did not have the capabilities required to deliver these services, and three service providers and their solutions were assessed during the decision-making process. Two of them were large global providers with solutions based on their 'standard' systems. The third was a small local provider with a customized, open-source solution.

Beta's risk assessment revealed that the solution which ended up being selected had the highest risk. Its risk score for issues related to the implementation were more than the other two combined and its risk score for issues related to maintenance was about 50 per cent more than the other two solutions. One of the main reasons for conducting the risk assessment was that the underlying business requirements were unclear and could not be codified to the extent where a third party could understand them, let alone implement them. Business requirements could be defined only conceptually; issues like facilitating collaboration, delivery management, knowledge management and even requirements for technical functions – 'Search', for instance – were not fully understood.

The selection of the service provider and the contract award process were based on a rather unorthodox approach, with strong evidence for

DOI: 10.1057/9781137497321.0010

trust-related attributes. The detailed requirement specifications were defined in close collaboration between Beta and the service provider. These details were then attached as an appendix to the contract. The implementation entailed collaborating to a large extent and the service provider was also selected because of its focus on understanding and fulfilling Beta's business needs, as opposed to the global providers, who focused more on marketing their existing solutions. Beta also preferred to utilize most of its investment on customizing its technical solution rather than on the acquisition of a standard system which was deemed to be incompatible with its requirements.

5.3.4   Analysis of trust and uncertainty

The infrastructure services outsourced are simple and can be codified and there is virtually no uncertainty associated with them. While there is an expectation and realization of high service levels at competitive pricing, there is also an excellent working relationship with the service provider. The IT manager confirms that there is no need for trust, although some attributes of performance-based and knowledge-based trust probably exist. He has a close relationship with key people in the service provider organization, and suggests that one can have person-to-person trust despite there not being any organization-to-organization trust. He also confirms that services like these are commodities and a contractual extension is not contingent on anything other than high service levels and competitive pricing.

However, the relationship with the portal service provider is far more relevant, which is why the analysis is limited to this one. This relationship is characterized by very high trust, and knowledge-based trust and identification-based trust are also present. It is a genuine partnership relationship. The analysis is aided considerably by the fact that the system owner and service coordinator, who participates in the case study, is also an experienced management consultant with academic qualifications which are very relevant for issues discussed in this study.

Trust had strong foundations and developed steadily over the course of the relationship. The service provider's focus on understanding Beta's needs from the outset contributed towards its development. Given the difficulty of being able to define and baseline requirements at the outset, both parties made a conscious decision to collaborate closely instead. Knowledge-based trust developed quickly and improved as both parties demonstrated their commitment. The contract has strong partnership

DOI: 10.1057/9781137497321.0010

characteristics and identification-based trust was engendered with shared objectives from the outset of the relationship. Both parties do significantly more than they are contractually obliged to, and very little in terms of roles and responsibilities are specified in this contract. The service provider's case was not driven only by contract profitability. They viewed the contract as an opportunity to build their capabilities and develop a solution which could be marketed to other clients. The contract reflected these benefits and Beta is eligible for royalties from sales of similar solutions to other clients.

There is a close relationship between key coordinators in both teams who have similar work culture and common country culture. He suggests that common culture matters and is an important factor in engendering trust and argues that cultural differences matter and that it is hard enough working in neighbouring countries, even when they are generally recognized as being similar to his own.

This, he argues is one of the reasons why it would be very difficult to collaborate with an offshore service provider. He argues that transaction costs would be significantly higher in such a situation and that search costs and contract management costs would be the smallest component. Most of the transaction costs, he suggests, would stem from internal coordination costs, and he rues the thought of fewer, or even no, face-to-face meetings, which are of great significance for him. Without these meetings coordination and communication would be harder and there would be little opportunity for the development of knowledge-based trust or personal relationships. He suggests that certain options would have been ruled out had it been an offshore provider due to the difficulty of face-to-face meetings.

On being asked to elaborate on concrete measures taken to engender trust, he argues that the most useful measure was meeting face-to-face. Not only does this help facilitating the contract, designing solutions and bridging gaps, it is also instrumental in engendering knowledge-based trust. He argues that trust develops only when people spend time together and that once trust has developed it is easier to sustain or strengthen it. He suggests that trust in the outsourcing relationship is influenced by firm culture, which holds that informal networks are at least as important as formal structure and argues that trust within his firm is often engendered by shared experiences. He argues that he has learned a great deal about his firm and colleagues on the golf course and in informal gatherings and cites examples of how his firm encourages and supports such activities.

DOI: 10.1057/9781137497321.0010

He suggests that Beta and its management value trust and place less emphasis on control than most other companies. He cites examples which would be unacceptable for companies which had a stronger control culture. He also suggests that there is even less control in functions within his firm than between Beta and the service provider.

On being asked to consider where trust and partnership could be less relevant, he suggests it is dependent on the nature of the services. The services in question do not have to be available 24–7, are not critical and are not client facing. Were this to be the case, he suggests then the need for control, reporting and codification would be higher, and it was far more unlikely to rely only on trust and collaboration.

Beta's outsourcing strategy is strongly influenced by trust and uncertainty. Despite the high uncertainty associated with the contract there was a deliberate decision to accept it at the outset and use trust as a means of addressing it. As in the previous case, this is strongly influenced by firm culture and service provider behaviour.

There is very low uncertainty in the relationship now (refer to Figure 5.2) and there is no market uncertainty. There is very little firm-related uncertainty, almost all of which is related to losing agility and flexibility due to the dependency on the service provider. But it was not always this way. There was high knowledge-related firm uncertainty and very high market uncertainty at the outset and there is a correlation between the reduction of these uncertainties and identification-based and knowledge-based trust.

The high search-related uncertainties at the outset were effectively reduced by a relationship with strong identification-based and knowledge-based trust. The firm's culture allowed it to accept the uncertainty of having to collaborate with a small outsourcing provider that was relatively unknown. The lack of knowledge was viewed as a potential source for competitiveness, despite the uncertainty. Enforcement-related trust manifested itself in drawing up a contract which at its core was little more than a page save the requirements, which were defined jointly. Trust is also manifested by neither party really referring to the contract, arguably because of its not being very enforceable. Control-related trust manifested itself in knowledge being shared proactively and openly from the outset. Communication was close and personal, with significant human interaction, and placed far more emphasis on humans than systems. There was very

DOI: 10.1057/9781137497321.0010

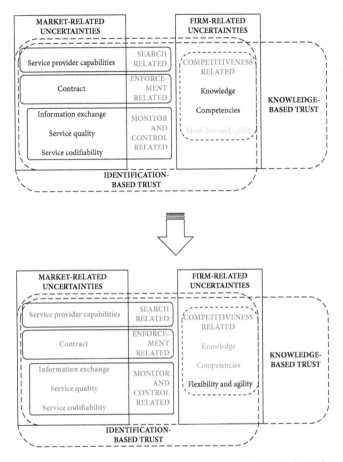

FIGURE 5.2   *Overview of uncertainty, its development with time and its relationship with trust*

Source: Authors' own.

close coordination and cooperation, which assumed the form of joint planning and joint action in a situation where the underlying service was not codifiable ex ante.

This approach is in stark contrast with the previous case and has clear benefits. There is high satisfaction with the performance of the service provider.

However, this situation could change in future. Beta's underlying business requirements are changing and competing providers now claim to offer superior standardized cloud-based solutions to meet these needs. While there is little uncertainty about the current service provider's ability to meet known requirements, there is more uncertainty related to its capability to meet unknown requirements in future, something competing global providers claim to do – and appear to provide evidence for – with conviction. Their solutions are based on cloud and commodity services. If they meet Beta's future requirements and are adopted, they will reduce uncertainty significantly and trust will no longer be as relevant as it is now.

5.4   Conclusions

There is a two-way causal relationship between trust and uncertainty in outsourcing. In situations of high uncertainty, trust can be engendered between service receivers and service providers to make outsourcing relationships materialize. In situations where it is not possible to generate trust between service receivers and service providers, measures can be taken to reduce uncertainty in order to take advantage of service provider capabilities.

In the first case study, the initial outsourcing decision is influenced by a low level of trust, which in turn is influenced by the service receiver's culture and its strong emphasis on control. The service receiver takes measures to reduce uncertainty by focusing on services, which are codifiable or commoditized, in order to maintain complete control of the services outsourced without having to rely on trust.

In the second case, the initial outsourcing decision is influenced by a high level of uncertainty. The service receiver and service provider take measures to engender trust from the outset to make the outsourcing relationship materialize and as a means of managing it. In this case the service receiver's culture is conducive to trust and there is far less emphasis on control, partly due to the nature of the service.

Both approaches have their merits and both approaches can be economically sound. Market-related outsourcing costs relate to search costs, contractual costs and transaction costs. In large outsourcing contracts, as in the first case, contractual costs can be calculated easily (the service provider fee) and usually comprise most of the costs. Transaction costs can be more difficult to estimate and estimates can

DOI: 10.1057/9781137497321.0010

be higher than the actual costs incurred. However, firms who avoid outsourcing due to this estimation being high stand to lose by not engaging in an outsourcing relationship if actual costs are lower than the estimates. Trust is a means of reducing these transactions costs and is beneficial to firms engaging in any outsourcing relationship.

DOI: 10.1057/9781137497321.0010

Conclusions

Datta, Surja and Neil Oschlag-Michael. *Understanding and Managing IT Outsourcing: A Partnership Approach.* Basingstoke: Palgrave Macmillan, 2015. DOI: 10.1057/9781137497321.0011.

▶

DOI: 10.1057/9781137497321.0011

This book advocates a partnership approach to outsourcing. But this statement needs to be qualified. Developing a partnership approach is a difficult process and not without risks. It has been suggested in this book that a partnership approach is most productive in outsourcing relationships that are characterized with a high level of uncertainty. This suggestion may sound paradoxical at the first instance. Firms tend to avoid uncertainty in outsourcing. When it is difficult to predict accurately what the future cost savings and gains in competitiveness are likely to be, firms typically prefer to 'make' instead of 'buy'. While this is a rational strategy, the book points to an alternate approach which is equally valid; one that is predicated on trust and hence on a partnership approach.

Uncertainty in outsourcing can signify both risk and reward, but in the absence of trust, market exchanges will not materialize, as firms will only appreciate the risks and not the potential rewards. In IT outsourcing, the potential bigger pay-offs for firms usually come from those instances where there is high uncertainty in terms of cost savings and gain in competitiveness but capturing them would require developing a partnership approach.

In advocating a partnership approach, this book also suggests where partnerships are far less relevant; namely, in situations where services are commoditized or codifiable. There is little, if any, uncertainty associated with these situations and it is unlikely that partnerships improve competitiveness or reduce costs.

DOI: 10.1057/9781137497321.0011

References

Akerlof, G.A. (1970) 'The market for "Lemons": Quality uncertainty and the market mechanism', *The Quarterly Journal of Economics*, Volume 84, Number 3.

Alexandrova, M. (2012) 'IT outsourcing partnerships: Empirical research on key success factors in Bulgarian organizations', *Management: Journal of Contemporary Management Issues*, Volume 17, Issue 2.

Armbrust, M., Fox, A., Griffith, R., Joseph, A. D., Katz, R., Konwinski, A., Lee, G., Patterson, D., Rabkin, A., Stoica, I. & Zaharia, M. (2009) *Above the Clouds: A Berkeley View of Cloud Computing*, UC Berkeley Reliable Adaptive Distributed Systems Laboratory, Available online at: http://www.cs.columbia.edu/~roxana/teaching/COMS-E6998-7-Fall-2011/papers/armbrust-tr09.pdf [Accessed on 3 March 2014].

Aronson, E. (1991) *The Social Animal*, W.H. Freeman and Company, New York.

Bachman, R. (2001) 'Trust, power and control in trans-organizational relations', *Organization Studies*, Volume 22, Number 2.

Barney, J.B. (1991) 'Firm resources and sustained competitive advantage', *Journal of Management*, Volume 17, Number 1.

Barney, J.B. (1999) 'How a firm's capabilities affect boundary decisions', *Sloan Management Review*, Spring.

Barney, J.B. & Lee, W. (1998) 'Governance under uncertainty: Transaction costs, real options, learning and property rights', Paper presented at the Annual Meeting of the Academy of Management.

DOI: 10.1057/9781137497321.0012

Beaumont, N. & Sohal, A. (2004) 'Outsourcing in Australia', *International Journal of Operations and Production Management*, Volume 24, Issue 7.

Beckert, J. (1996) 'What is sociological about economic sociology? Uncertainty and the embeddedness of economic action', *Theory and Society*, Volume 25, Number 6.

Beckman, C.M., Haunschild, P.R. & Phillips, D.J. (2004) 'Friends or strangers? Firm specific uncertainty, market uncertainty and network partner selection', *Organization Science*, Volume 15, Number 3.

Bekmamedova, N., Prananto, A., McKay, J. & Vorobiev, A. (2008) 'Towards a conceptualisation of trust in IS Outsourcing', *Association for Information Systems*.

Bowman, E.H. & Hurry, D. (1993) 'Strategy through the option lens: An integrated view of resource investments and the incremental choice process', *The Academy of Management Review*, Volume 18, Number 4.

Brinkkemper, S. & Jansen, S. (2012) 'Collaboration in Outsourcing – A Journey to Quality' Pa Burt, R. 2005, Brokerage and Closure: An Introduction to Social Capital, Oxford University Press, New York.

Burt, R. (1980) 'Models of network structure', *Annual Review of Sociology*, Volume 6, Palgrave Macmillan.

Burt, R. (1992) *Structural Holes: The Social Structure of Competition*, Harvard University Press, Cambridge, MA.

Burt, R. (1997) 'The contingent value of social capital', *Administrative Science Quarterly*, Volume 42.

Burt, R. (2000) 'The Network Structure of Social Capital' in *Research in Organizational Behaviour*, Volume 22, eds Staw, B.M. & Sutton, R.L., Elsevier Science Inc., New York.

Burt, R. (2004) 'Structural holes and good ideas', *American Journal of Sociology*, Volume 110, Number 2.

Chadee, D. & Raman, R. (2009) 'International outsourcing of information technology services: Review and future directions', *International Marketing Review*, Volume 26, Issue 4/5.

Chandler, A.D. (1977) *The Visible Hand: The Managerial Revolution in American Business*, Belknap Press, Cambridge, MA.

Cheon, M.J., Grover, V. & Teng, J.T.C. (1995) 'Theoretical perspectives on the outsourcing of information systems', *Journal of Information Technology*, Volume 10, Issue 4.

Civilis, E. (2013) 'Rethinking vendor's local capabilities: Enabling business value realization in IT outsourcing', [a dissertation

DOI: 10.1057/9781137497321.0012

submitted in part-fulfilment of the requirements for the degree of Master of Business Administration of the University of Warwick].

Coase, R. (1937) 'The nature of the firm', *Economica*, Volume 4, Number 3.

Cohen, M.D. & Bacdayan, P. (1994) 'Organizational routines are stored as procedural memory: Evidence from a laboratory study', *Organization Science*, Volume 5, Number 4, pp. 554–68.

Coleman, J.S. (1986) 'Social theory, social research, and a theory of action', *American Journal of Sociology*, Volume 91, Number 6, pp. 1309–35.

Cox, M., Roberts, M. & Walton, J. (2011) 'IT outsourcing in the public sector: Experiences from local government', *Electronic Journal of Information Systems Evaluation*, Volume 14, Issue 2.

Dasgupta, P. (1988) 'Trust as a commodity' in *Trust: Making and breaking cooperative relations,* ed Gambetta, D. Basil Blackwell [cited in Gainey, T.W. and Klaas, B.S. (2003) 'The outsourcing of training and development: Factors impacting client satisfaction', *Journal of Management*, Volume: 29, Issue: 2].

Deloitte (2012) '2012 Global Outsourcing and Insourcing Survey', Available online at: http://www.deloitte.com/assets/Dcom-UnitedStates/Local%20Assets/Documents/IMOs/Shared%20 Services/us_sdt_2012GlobalOutsourcingandInsourcingSurveyExecut iveSummary_050112.pdf [Accessed on 17 February 2013].

Deloitte (2013) 'The Cloud and Outsourcing: A New World Awaits', Available online at: http://deloitte.wsj.com/cio/2013/01/14/the-cloud-and-outsourcing-a-new-world-awaits/ [Accessed on 17 February 2013].

Dibbern, J., Goles, T., Hirschheim, R. & Jayatilaka, B. (2004) "Information systems outsourcing: A survey and analysis of the literature", *The DATA BASE for Advances in Information Systems*, Volume 34, Issue 4.

Dorsch, M. J., Swanson, S. R. & Kelley, S.W. (1998) 'The role of relationship quality in the stratification of vendors as perceived by customers', *Academy of Marketing Science*, Volume 26 [cited in Gainey, T.W. and Klaas, B.S. (2003) 'The outsourcing of training and development: Factors impacting client satisfaction', *Journal of Management*, Volume 29, Issue 2].

Duffy, R.S. (2008) 'Towards a better understanding of partnership attributes: An exploratory analysis of relationship type classification', *Industrial Marketing Management*, Volume 37, Issue 2.

Dyer, J. (1997) 'Effective inter-firm collaboration: How firms minimize transaction costs and maximize transaction value', *Strategic Management Journal*, Volume 18, Issue 7.

Dyer, J. H. & Chu, W. (2003) 'The role of trustworthiness in reducing transaction costs and improving performance: Empirical evidence from the United States, Japan, and Korea', *Organization Science*, Volume 14, Issue 1.

Economist (2014) 'Special report: Tech start-ups' January 18th edition.

Eisenhardt, K.M. (1989) 'Building theories from case study research', *The Academy of Management Review*, Volume 14, Number 4, Available online at: http://www.jstor.org/stable/258557 [Accessed on 3 March 2014].

Eisenhardt, K.M. & Graebner, M.E. (2007) 'Theory building from cases: Opportunities and challenges', *Academy of Management Journal*, Volume 50, Number 1.

Feeny, D. and Willcocks, L. (1998) 'Core IT capabilities for exploiting information technology', *Sloan Management Review*, Volume 39, Issue 3.

Feeny, D., Willcocks, L. & Lacity, M. (2003) 'Business process outsourcing: The promise of the 'enterprise partnership' model', *Templeton Executive Briefing*, Templeton College, University of Oxford. Available online at: http://www.carig.co.uk/pages/userdata/carig/bpoenterprisepartnership_teb.pdf [Accessed on 3 March 2013].

Feeny, D., Lacity, M. & Willcocks, L. (2005) 'Taking the measure of outsourcing service providers', *Sloan Management Review*, Volume 46, Issue 3.

Fish, K.E. & Seydel, J. (2006) 'Where IT outsourcing is and where it is going: A study across functions and department sizes', *Journal of Computer Information Systems*, Volume 46, Issue 3.

Fisher, S.R. & White, M.A. (2000) 'Downsizing in a learning organization: Are there hidden costs?', *The Academy of Management Review*, Volume 25, Number 1.

Fitzgerald, G. & Willcocks, L.P. (1994) 'Relationships in outsourcing: Contracts and partnerships', in *ECIS* (pp. 51–66), Second European Conference on Information Systems, Nijenrode University, The Netherlands. Available online at: http://csrc.lse.ac.uk/asp/aspecis/19940051.pdf [Accessed on 25 September 2013].

Freeman, S.J. & Cameron, K.S. (1993) 'Organizational downsizing: A convergence and reorientation framework', *Organization Science*, Volume 4, Number 1.

DOI: 10.1057/9781137497321.0012

Gainey, T.W. & Klaas, B.S. (2003) 'The outsourcing of training and development: Factors impacting client satisfaction', *Journal of Management*, Volume 29, Issue 2.

Gartner (2013) *IT Outsourcing*, Available online at: http://www.gartner.com/it-glossary/it-outsourcing [Accessed on 25 November 2013].

Gartner (2014) *Special report: Cloud computing*, Available online at: http://www.gartner.com/technology/research/cloud-computing/report/cloud-sourcing.jsp [Accessed on 3 March 2014].

Golembiewski, R.T. & McConkie, M. (1975) *The Centrality of Interpersonal Trust in Group Processes*, John Wiley and Sons.

Granovetter, M. (1985) 'Economic action and social structure: The problem of embeddedness', *American Journal of Sociology*, Volume 91.

Granovetter, M. (1990) 'The Old and the New Economic Sociology: A History and an Agenda' in *Beyond the Marketplace: Rethinking Economy and Society*, eds Friedland, R. & Robertson, A.F., Aldine Transaction, New York.

Granovetter, M. (1999) 'Coase encounters and formal models: Taking Gibbons seriously', *Administrative Science Quarterly*, Volume 44, Number 1.

Granovetter, M. (2005) 'The impact of social structure on economic outcomes', *The Journal of Economic Perspectives*, Volume 19, Number 1.

Gottschalk, P. & Solli-Saether, H. (2005) 'Critical success factors from IT outsourcing theories: An empirical study', *Industrial Management & Data Systems*, 105(5–6).

Grover, V., Cheon, M.J. & Teng, J.T. (1996) 'The effect of service quality and partnership on the outsourcing of information systems functions', *Journal of Management Information Systems*, Volume 12, Issue 4.

Gulati, R. (1995) 'Does familiarity breed trust? The implications of repeated ties for contractual choice in alliances', *Academy of Management Journal*, Volume 38, Number 1.

Hamel, G. & Prahalad, C.K. (1990) 'The core competencies of the corporation', *Harvard Business Review*, May–June.

Hancox, M. & Hackney, R. (2000) 'IT outsourcing: Frameworks for conceptualizing practice and perception', *Information Systems Journal*, Volume 10, Number 3.

Henderson, J.C. (1990) 'Plugging into strategic partnerships: The critical IS connection', *Sloan Management Review*, Volume 30, Number 3.

DOI: 10.1057/9781137497321.0012

Hodgson, G. (2006) 'What are institutions?', *Journal of Economic Issues*, Volume XL, Number 1.

Huxham, C. & Vangen, S. (2003) 'Nurturing collaborative relations: Building trust in interorganizational collaboration', *Journal of Applied Behavioural Science*, Volume 39, Number 1.

IBM.com (2114) '[Services]', Available online at: http://www.ibm.com/us/en/ [Accessed on 12 December 2014].

Ishikaza, A. & Blakiston, R. (2012) 'The 18 C model for a successful long-term outsourcing arrangement', *Industrial Marketing Management*, Number 41, 1071–80.

Jankowicz, A.D. (2004) 'Business Research Projects', 4th edn., Cengage Learning Business Press, London, cited in BPP Learning Media (2013), "Research Methods".

Johanson, J. & Vahlne, J.E. (1977) 'The internationalization process of the firm: A model of knowledge development and increasing foreign commitments', *Journal of International Business Studies*, Volume 8, Number 1.

Jones, C., Hesterly, W.S. & Borgatti, S.P. (1997) 'A general theory of network governance: Exchange conditions and social mechanisms', *Academy of Management Review*, Volume 22, Number 4.

Kanter, R. (1994) 'Collaborative advantage, the art of alliances', *Harvard Business Review*, Volume 72, Number 4, July–August.

Kavcic, K. & Tavcar, M. I. (2008) 'Planning successful partnership in the process of outsourcing', *Kybernetes*, Volume 37, Issue 2.

Kedia, B. L. & Lahiri, S. (2007) 'International outsourcing of services: A partnership model', *Journal of International Management*, Volume 13, Issue 1.

Kern, T. & Willcocks, L. (2000) 'Exploring information technology outsourcing relationships: Theory and practice', *Journal of Strategic Information Systems*, Volume 9, Issue 4.

Kishore, R., Rao, H., Nam, K., Rajagopalan, S. & Chaudhury, A. (2003) 'A relationship perspective on IT outsourcing', *Communications of the ACM*, Volume 46, Issue 12.

Knight, F. (1921) *Risk, Uncertainty and Profit*, Hart, Schaffner & Marx, Houghton Mifflin Company, Boston, MA.

Kogut, B. & Zander, U. (1992) 'Knowledge of the firm, combinative capabilities and the replication of technology', *Organization Science*, Volume 3, Number 3.

DOI: 10.1057/9781137497321.0012

Konsynski, B. R. & McFarlan, E. (1990) 'Information partnerships–
Shared data, shared scale', *Harvard Business Review*, Volume 68,
Issue 5.

Korrapati, R.B. (2009) 'Risks and success factors in information
technology (IT) outsourcing', Proceedings of the Academy
of Information and Management Sciences, Allied Academies
International Conference, January 1.

Krackhardt, D. (1990) 'Assessing the political landscape: Structure,
cognition, and power in organizations', *Administrative Science
Quarterly*, Volume 35.

Krackhardt, D. & Hanson, J. (1993) 'Informal networks: The
company behind the chart', *Harvard Business Review*, Volume 71,
Number 4.

Lacity, M.C. & Willcocks, L.P. (2014) 'Business process outsourcing and
dynamic innovation', *Strategic Outsourcing: An International Journal*,
Volume 7, Issue 1.

Lacity, M.C. & Willcocks, L.P. (2008) *Offshore Outsourcing of IT Work*,
Palgrave Macmillan.

Lacity, M.C. & Willcocks, L.P. (2000) 'Relationships in IT outsourcing:
A stakeholder perspective', in *Framing the Domains of IT Management:
Projecting the Future through the Past*, ed Zmud, R.W., Pinnaflex
Educational Resources, Cincinnati, OH, 355–84.

Lacity, M.C. & Willcocks, L.P. (1998) 'An empirical investigation
of information technology outsourcing practices: Lessons from
experience', *MIS Quarterly*, Volume 22, Issue 3.

Lacity, M.C., Willcocks, L.P. & Feeny, D. F. (1996) 'The value of selective
IT sourcing', *Sloan Management Review*, Volume 37, Issue 3.

Lane, C. & Bachman, R. (1996) 'The social construction of supplier
relation in Britain and Germany', *Organization Studies*, Volume 17,
Number 3.

Lee, J.N. (2001) 'The impact of knowledge sharing, organizational
capability and partnership quality on IS outsourcing success',
Information and Management, Volume 38, Issue 5.

Lee, J. N., Huynh, M.Q., Chi-wai, K.R. & Pi, S.M. (2000) 'The evolution
of outsourcing research: What is the next issue?', in *System Sciences*,
2000. Proceedings of the 33rd Annual Hawaii International
Conference on Systems Sciences (pp. 1-10). IEEE. Available online at:
http://citeseerx.ist.psu.edu/viewdoc/download?doi=10.1.1.96.6507&re
p=rep1&type=pdf [Accessed on 25 September 2013].

DOI: 10.1057/9781137497321.0012

Lee, J.N., Huynh, M.Q., Kwok, R. C-W. & Pi, S-M. (2003) 'IT outsourcing evolution – past, present, and future', *Communications of the ACM*, Volume 46, Issue 5.

Lee, J.N. & Kim, Y-G. (1999) 'Effect of partnership quality on IS outsourcing success: Conceptual framework and empirical validation', *Journal of Management Information Systems*, Volume 15, Issue 4.

Lee, N. & Kim, Y.G. (2005) 'Understanding outsourcing partnership: A comparison of three theoretical perspectives', *Engineering Management*, IEEE Transactions on, Volume 52, Issue 4.

Lewicki, R.J. & Bunker, B.B. (1996) 'Developing and maintaining trust in work relationships', in *Trust in organizations: Frontiers of theory and research*, eds Kramer, R. M. & Tyler, T.R., Sage Publications.

Lewicki, R.J., McAllister, D.J. & Bies, R.J. (1998) 'Trust and distrust: New relationships and realities', *Academy of Management Review*, Volume 23 [cited in Gainey, T.W. and Klaas, B.S. (2003) 'The outsourcing of training and development: Factors impacting client satisfaction', *Journal of Management*, Volume 29, Issue 2].

Lin, N. (2001) *Social Capital: A Theory of Social Structure and Action*, Cambridge University Press, New York.

Lovelock, C.H. (1992) *Managing Services*, Prentice Hall, Englewood Cliffs, NJ.

Maguire, S., Phillips, N. & Hardy, C. (2001) 'When 'Silence=Death', Keep Talking: Trust, Control and Discursive Construction of Identity in the Canadian HIV/AIDS Treatment Domain', *Organization Studies*, Volume 22, Number 2.

Mascarenhas, B. (1982) 'Coping with uncertainty in international business', *Journal of International Business Studies*, Volume 13, Number 2.

McKnight, D.H. & Chervany, N.L. (1996) 'The Meanings of Trust', *Technical Report*, University of Minnesota [cited in Bekmamedova, N., Prananto, A., McKay, J. & Vorobiev, A. (2008) 'Towards a conceptualisation of trust in IS outsourcing', *Association for Information Systems*].

Mehta, N. & Mehta, A. (2010) 'It takes two to Tango: How relational investments improve outsourcing partnerships', *Communications of the ACM*, Volume 53, Issue 2.

Miller, K.D. (1992) 'A framework for integrated risk management in international business', *Journal of International Business Studies*, Volume 23, Number 2.

DOI: 10.1057/9781137497321.0012

Mintzberg, H., Ahlstrand, B. & Lampel, J. (1998) *Strategy Safari: A Guided Tour through the Wilds of Strategic Management*, The Free Press, New York.

Miranda, S.M. & Kavan, C.B. (2005) 'Moments of governance in IS outsourcing: Conceptualising effects of contracts on value capture and creation', *Journal of Information Technology*, Volume 20, June.

Mohr, J. & Spekman, R. (1994) 'Characteristics of partnership success: Partnership attributes, Communication behaviour and conflict resolution techniques', *Strategic Management Journal*, Volume 15, Issue 2.

Moran, P. & Ghoshal, S. (1999) 'Markets, firms, and the process of economic development', *The Academy of Management Review*, Volume 24, Number 3.

Nahapiet, J. & Ghoshal, S. (1998) 'Social capital, intellectual capital, and the organizational advantage', *The Academy of Management Review*, Volume 23, Number 2.

Nelson, R. & Winter, S. (1982) *An Evolutionary Theory of Economic Change*, The Belknap Press of Harvard University Press, MA.

North, D.C. (1990) *Institutions, Institutional Change and Economic Performance*, Cambridge University Press, Cambridge.

North, D.C. (1991) 'Institutions', *Journal of Economic Perspectives*, Volume 5, Number 1.

Ohmae, K. (1982) *The Mind of the Strategist*, McGraw Hill, New York.

Oshri, I. & Kotlarsky, J. (2009) 'Realising the real benefits of outsourcing', *Warwick Business School Report*.

Oshri, I., Kotlarsky, J. & Willcocks, L. (2008) *Outsourcing Global Services Knowledge: Innovation and Social Capital*, Palgrave Macmillan.

Oshri, I., Kotlarsky, J. & Willcocks, L. (2009) *The Handbook of Global Outsourcing and Offshoring*, Palgrave Macmillan.

Oviatt, B.M. & McDougall, P.P. (1994) 'Towards a theory of international new ventures', *Journal of International Business Studies*, Volume 25.

Patel, A. & Aran, H. (2005) *Outsourcing Success: The Management Imperative*, Palgrave Macmillan [cited in Poppo, L. & Zenger, T. (2002) 'Do formal contracts and relational governance function as substitutes or complements?', *Strategic Management Journal*, Volume 23, Issue 8].

Paul, D.L. & McDaniel, J.R. (2004) 'A field study of the effect of interpersonal trust on virtual collaborative relationship performance', *MIS Quarterly*, Volume 28, Issue 2, [cited in Bekmamedova, N., Prananto, A., McKay, J. & Vorobiev, A. (2008) 'Towards

DOI: 10.1057/9781137497321.0012

a conceptualisation of trust in IS outsourcing', *Association for Information Systems*].

Piore, M.J. (1992) 'Fragments of a cognitive theory of technological change and organizational structure', in *Networks and Organizations: Structure, Form, and Action*, eds Nohria, N. & Eccles, R.G., Harvard Business School Press, Boston, MA.

Podolny, J.M. & Page, K.L. (1998) 'Network forms of organization', *Annual Review of Sociology*, Volume 24.

Porter, M.E. (1980) *Competitive Strategy*, Free Press, New York.

Prananto, A., McKay, J. & Vorobiev, A. (2008) 'Towards a conceptualisation of trust in IS outsourcing', *Association for Information Systems*.

Putnam, R.D. (2000) *Bowling Alone: The Collapse and Revival of American Community*, Simon and Schuster, New York.

Quinn, J.B. (1992) *Intelligent Enterprise*, The Free Press, New York.

Quinn, J.B. (1999) 'Strategic outsourcing: Leveraging knowledge capabilities', *Sloan Management Review*, Volume 40, Number 4.

Quinn, J., Brian & Hilmer, F.G. (1994) 'Strategic outsourcing', *Sloan Management Review*, Summer.

Rangan, S. (2000) 'The problem of search and deliberation in economic action: When social networks really matter', *The Academy of Management Review*, Volume 25, Number 4.

Rousseau, D.M., Sitkin, S.B., Burt, R.S. & Camerer, C. (1988) 'Not so different after all: A cross-discipline view of trust', *Academy of Management Review*, Volume 23, Issue 3, [cited in Bekmamedova, N., Prananto, A., McKay, J. & Vorobiev, A. (2008) 'Towards a conceptualisation of trust in IS outsourcing', *Association for Information Systems*].

Sabherwal, R. (1999) 'The role of trust in outsourced IS development projects', *Communication of the ACM*, Volume 42, Issue 2.

Saparito, P.A., Chen, C.C. & Sapienza, H.J. (2004) 'The role of relational trust in bank small-firm relationships', *Academy of Management Journal*, Volume 47, Issue 3, [cited in Bekmamedova, N., Prananto, A., McKay, J. & Vorobiev, A. (2008) 'Towards a conceptualisation of trust in IS outsourcing', *Association for Information Systems*].

Saunders, M., Thornhill, A. & Lewis, P. (2013) *Research Methods for Business Students*, 6th edn., Electronic edition, Pearson.

Saxenian, A. (2002) 'Brain circulation: How high-skill immigration makes everyone better off', *The Brookings Review*, Volume 20, Number 1.

DOI: 10.1057/9781137497321.0012

Saxenian, A. (2005) 'From brain drain to brain circulation: Transnational communities and regional upgrading in India and China', *Studies in Comparative International Development (SCID)*, Volume 40, Number 1.

Searle, J. (2005) 'What is an institution?', *Journal of Institutional Economics*, Volume 1, Number 1.

Shapiro, D.L., Sheppard, B.H. & Cheraskin, L. (1992) 'Business on a handshake', *Negotiation Journal*, Volume 8, Issue 4, [cited in Bekmamedova, N., Prananto, A., McKay, J. & Vorobiev, A. (2008) 'Towards a conceptualisation of trust in IS outsourcing', *Association for Information Systems*].

Shapiro, S.P. (1987) 'The social control of impersonal trust', *The American Journal of Sociology*, Volume 93, Number 3.

Simon, H. (1955) 'A behavioural model of rational choice', *The Quarterly Journal of Economics*, Volume 69, Number 1.

Simon, H.A. (1991) 'Bounded rationality and organizational learning', *Organization Science*, Volume 2, Number 1.

Spekman, R.E., Kamauff, J.W., Jr & Myhr, N. (1998) 'An empirical investigation into supply chain management: A perspective on partnerships', *Supply Chain Management*, Volume 3, Issue 2.

Spender, J.C. (1996) 'Making knowledge the basis of a dynamic theory of the firm', *Strategic Management Journal*, Volume 17, Number [*Special Issue: Knowledge and the Firm*].

Sun, S.Y., Lin, T.C. & Sun, P.C. (2002) 'The factors influencing information systems outsourcing partnership – a study integrating case study and survey research methods', in *System Sciences*, HICSS. Proceedings of the 35th Annual Hawaii International Conference on (pp. 2810–9). IEEE. Available online at: http://140.127.194.87:8080/ECLab/paper%20 set/8rd/0821–2.pdf [Accessed on 25 September 2013].

Tafti, M.H.A. (2005) 'Risk factors associated with offshore IT outsourcing', *Industrial Management & Data Systems*, Volume 105, Number 5.

TCS.com (2114) 'Services', Available online at: http://www.tcs.com/ offerings/Pages/default.aspx [Accessed on 12 December 2013].

Teece, D., Pisano, G. & Shuen, A. (1997) 'Dynamic capabilities and strategic management', *Strategic Management Journal*, Volume 18, Number 7.

Thomson, J.D. (1967) *Organizations in Actions*, McGraw-Hill, New York.

DOI: 10.1057/9781137497321.0012

Tsai, W. & Ghoshal, S. (1998) 'Social capital and value creation: The role of intrafirm networks', *The Academy of Management Journal*, Volume 41, Number 4.

Tversky, A. & Kahneman, D. (1974) 'Judgment under uncertainty: Heuristics and biases', *Science*, Volume 185.

Uzzi, B. (1997) 'Social structure and competition in interfirm networks: The paradox of embeddedness', *Administrative Science Quarterly*, Volume 42.

Vitasek, K. & Manrodt, K. (2012) 'Vested outsourcing – a flexible framework for collaborative outsourcing', *Strategic Outsourcing: An International Journal*, Volume 5, Issue 1.

Whitley, E.A. & Willcocks, L. (2011) 'Achieving step-change in outsourcing maturity: Toward collaborative innovation', *MIS Quarterly Executive*, Volume 10, Issue 3.

Whittington, R. (2001) *What Is Strategy – and Does It Matter?*, 2nd edn, Thomas Learning.

Williamson, O.E. (1979) 'The governance of contractual relations', *Journal of Law and Economics*, Volume 22.

Williamson, O.E. (1985) *The Economic Institutions of Capitalism*, The Free Press, New York.

Willcocks, L. & Choi, C. J. (1995) 'Co-operative partnership and "total" IT outsourcing: from contractual obligation to strategic alliance?' *European Management Journal*, Volume 13, Issue 1.

Willcocks, L.P., Cullen, S. & Craig, A. (2011) *The Outsourcing Enterprise: From Cost Management to Collaborative Innovation*, Palgrave Macmillan.

Willcocks, L. P. & Lacity, M. C. (2006) *Global Sourcing of Business and IT Services*, Palgrave Macmillan.

Willcocks, L.P. & Lacity, M.C. (2009) *The Practice of Outsourcing – from Information Systems to BPO and Offshoring*, Palgrave Macmillan.

DOI: 10.1057/9781137497321.0012

Index

DOI: 10.1057/9781137497321.0013

DOI: 10.1057/9781137497321.0013

GPSR Compliance
The European Union's (EU) General Product Safety Regulation (GPSR) is a set
of rules that requires consumer products to be safe and our obligations to
ensure this.

If you have any concerns about our products, you can contact us on

ProductSafety@springernature.com

In case Publisher is established outside the EU, the EU authorized
representative is:

Springer Nature Customer Service Center GmbH
Europaplatz 3
69115 Heidelberg, Germany